Fly-Fishing
ALASKA'S
WILD RIVERS

by Dan Heiner

STACKPOLE
BOOKS

Published by
STACKPOLE BOOKS
5067 Ritter Road
Mechanicsburg, Pennsylvania 17055

Portions of the material in this book appeared previously in Dan Heiner's books
Alaska on the Fly, and *In Search of Alaska's Best Fly-Fishing.*

Fly Drawings by Jon Conrad/Jon Conrad Studio, Monrovia, CA
Line Drawings by James Havens/Wasilla, AK
Watercolor Painting by C. D. Clarke/P.O. Box 344, Upper Fairmount, MD
Fly Pattern Photos by Greg Martin/Greg Martin Photography, Anchorage, AK
All other photos by Dan Heiner, unless otherwise credited
Map illustrations by Wendy A. Reynolds and Caroline M. Stover

Printed in the United States of America

10 9 8 7 6 5 4 3 2

First Edition

Library of Congress Cataloging-in-Publication Data

Heiner, Dan.
    Fly-fishing Alaska's wild rivers / Dan Heiner.
       p. cm.
    ISBN 0-8117-2762-9
    1. Fly fishing—Alaska—Guidebooks. 2. Freshwater fishes—Alaska.
    3. Alaska—Guidebooks. I. Title.
    SH467.H45 1998
    799.1'1'09798—dc21   97-29137
                                       CIP

This book is dedicated to my father,
Daniel P. Heiner,
for teaching me, among other things, to fly-fish,
and also to the memory of
Tom Bukowski

W hatever you can do, or dream you can, begin it.
Boldness has genius, power, and magic in it.
—Goethe

ACKNOWLEDGMENTS

At the risk of forgetting several individuals, I'd like to thank the following people for their inspiration and assistance over the years:

my wife, Anne Heiner, Steve and Gina Abel, R. Clark Alvey, Nick Amato, Geoff Armstrong, Lem Batchelder, Mark and Greg Bell, Bo Bennett, Mike Bergt, Ken Bethe, Doug and Danny Brewer, Eberhard Brunner, David Byrne, Jimmy Carlsen, Dr. Joseph Leon Chandler, Jack Charlton, Peter Cockwill, Trey Combs, Jon Conrad, Tom Coomer, Bob Couey, Bob Cusack, Dr. Mike Cusack, Dale DePriest, Bobby DeVito, Jerry Donaldson, John Donovan, Mike Dooley, Claire Dubbin, David Ford, Dennis Gearhart, Ted and Mary Gerken, John Gierach, Gus Gillispie, Jeff and Don Glaser, Chris Goll, Mike Gorton, Greg Hamm, Wayne Hansen, Greg Harrington, Jack Harris, Van Hartley, Tom Haugen, Albert P. Heiner, Mike Hershberger, Bill Herzog, Bob and Jed Holley, John Hutchinson, Ron Hyde, Sr., Les Jacober, Eric Jameson, Lawrence John, Bruce Johnson, Mark Johnson, Ray Johnson, Will Johnson, Elly Jones, Randall Kaufmann, Bob Keller, Craig Ketchum, Gary King, Jr., Russ King, John Klar, Greg Lindgren, John and Joyce Logan, Gary Loomis, Ames Luce, Andy MacLeod, Bob Marriott, Greg Martin, Sean McAdams, Dennis McAffee, Dennis and Sharon McCracken, Dr. David McGuire, Thomas E. McGuire, Don Meahan, Michael Mills, Perry Mollan, Nanci Morris, Willie Morris, Greg Niesen, Russ Nogg, Bernie Ortman, John Ortman, Jr., John Ortman, Sr., Mike Patton, Gunnar Pedersen, Raymond "Sonny" Petersen, Ray Petersen, Sr., Kip Roberti, Paul "Eli" Rotkis, Mike Sanders, Tony Sarp, Marty Sherman, Chris Smith, Franklin "Doc" Smith, Larry Smith, John Stacer, Bob Stearns, Dick Steinman, John Sumrall, Evan Swensen, Jim Teeny, Bret and Mark

Thunell, Bob and Curt Trout, Tony Weaver, Tom White, Bob Whitten-berg, Jimmy Winchester, Rod Wolfrum, Dick and Darwin Wright, and the many Alaska fishing guides, pilots, and clients I have been privileged to spend time with. Special appreciation also to Harry Geron, antique tackle advisor, Vera de'Clair, Professional Processing, G. Loomis, Inc.

CONTENTS

PART FOUR: THE FISH AND THE FISHING

FOREWORD

Alaska's residents give their place of worship as "AK" the way less advantaged mortals say "USA," they still consider moose one of the basic food groups, and they know in their souls that their lands ultimately define cold-water fly fishing. This is less a matter of smugness than why they have chosen to be Alaskans. Their salmon are either the largest or most abundant on earth and annually become migratory spectacles of continental proportions. Their rainbow trout fishery simply has no equal on this planet. Their grayling, arctic char, and sheefish take turns at being symbols of Alaska's wildness.

Many writers have successfully chronicled the magnitude of this fishery, but precious few have tellingly explained what it means to be both an Alaskan and a fly fisher. Dan Heiner has succeeded on both accounts in *Fly-Fishing Alaska's Wild Rivers*. He takes us on an intimate journey from sparkling waters and rising trout to bears and bush planes. He believes he can do this only when in good company. Sweet camaraderie is Dan's full creel. He measures each day in that manner, a perspective that invariably gives his stories depth and gentle humor.

I first met Dan on the Alagnak River late into a dry-fly spring. We moused in the braids, cast tiny drys on the flats when the caddis rained down, and waked Humpies over the big tailouts. The rainbow fishing was good, the days magical. Dan, the talented angler, became the consummate friend. I found that his self-deprecating humor and contagious laughter made for jolly times regardless of weather or circumstances. During the years since, we fished Alaska together, at one time or another every month, June to mid–October, and I never had a better companion

or a more knowledgeable teacher. I believe that those anglers who read
Fly-Fishing Alaska's Wild Rivers will feel much the same.

—Trey Combs
Contributing Editor, *Fly Fisherman*

IF THERE'S ANY FRESHWATER FLY-FISHING EXPERIENCE THAT is more exciting than venturing off to the wilds of Alaska for a go at trophy rainbow trout, or arctic grayling, or arctic char, or, for that matter, any of the Great Land's thirteen sportfish species, I'd like to know about it.

Whether you hop a float plane and fly off to one of Alaska's premier wilderness fisheries or simply climb into an automobile and drive to a roadside location, fly-fishing Alaska can be magical.

There is a certain feeling a fly fisher gets when he's standing out in one of Alaska's wild rivers. Chasing rainbows, I call it. I'm not certain where the feeling comes from, if it has to do with Alaska itself, its numbers of fish (including five species of Pacific salmon), or the size of the fish, but it's there, a feeling of electricity combined with a flow of adrenaline that simply goes with *being* in the Great Land. It's a feeling that's difficult to describe, but it's real, and it has caused more than a few fly fishers to relocate to the forty-ninth state just so they can be that much nearer the fishing.

Alaska's fly fishers don't need to sample more than a handful of the Last Frontier's rivers or fish species before they find themselves addicted to the place and its wild rivers, and feeling compelled to explore other remote fisheries, never mind the obstacles in getting there.

Those who have experienced Alaska know the Great Land can form vivid, indelible memories: the remote wilderness rivers and streams, the myriad birds and wildlife, the snowcapped mountains reflecting off the water's surface, the stands of dark, spindly Alaska spruce silhouetted

1

against a distant midnight sun. To many, the Alaska experience means seeing a bear wandering along a riverbank, or a pair of bald eagles circling overhead, or a lone moose peering down from the alders. And for Alaska fly fishers, it's the numbers and the sizes of the fish. For dry-fly fishers, it's the sight of those dimpled rings scattered across the surface of premier waters. Truth is, just being in Alaska's remote wilderness (away from automobiles, pollution, parking meters, and the pressures of everyday life) is reason enough to develop a love affair with the state.

The very magnitude of the forty-ninth state lets fly fishers experience virtually undisturbed backcountry lakes and pristine wilderness streams that remain much as they've existed for centuries—places with hardly a sign of man's presence or his wastes. But a word of caution: There really is no such thing as a once-in-a-lifetime Alaska fly-fishing experience. Most anglers who do venture off to the north country nearly always return. For what fly fisher of any conviction can resist the Great Land's ultimate waters before he's ready to put away his fly rod and quit fly-fishing the Alaska of his dreams?

Ah, yes, *Alyeska*—the Great Land! It can be magical experience, all right. Add a good partner to share it with, and you've really got something.

Fly-Fishing Alaska's Wild Rivers was written primarily around my affinity for pursuing rainbow trout with a fly. Each of the Great Land's thirteen other sportfish species are covered fairly extensively in this book; however, after considering the immense size of the state, I decided to focus on the premier rainbow trout/char/salmon rivers found in the southwestern region of the state, the area commonly referred to as the Bristol Bay Sportfishing Region.

Readers will also note that several of Alaska's real-life individuals and fishing lodges are mentioned throughout the text. Not only is this an attempt to bring Alaska to life, but fishing lodges also serve as the only landmarks in many of Alaska's vast unpopulated regions.

I am a believer that above all else, fly fishing should provide enjoyment. Although I take fly-fishing Alaska seriously, I try not to take it *too* seriously. For me, fly-fishing Alaska is an all-encompassing adventure, not a scientific endeavor.

Please join me, if you will, as I visit the premier Alaska waters I've been fortunate enough to have experienced over the past decade. I'll do my best to bring Alaska to life by describing Alaska's fish species and its fishing, relating a few personal vignettes and some about others as well. I hope you'll want to come and visit and sample for yourself some of the wonders of the Great Land.

So, come on! Let's climb in and buckle up. The pilot has just finished pumping out the floats, and the look in his eye tells me we're about ready to take off on yet another exciting Alaska fly-fishing adventure.

PART ONE

Getting Ready

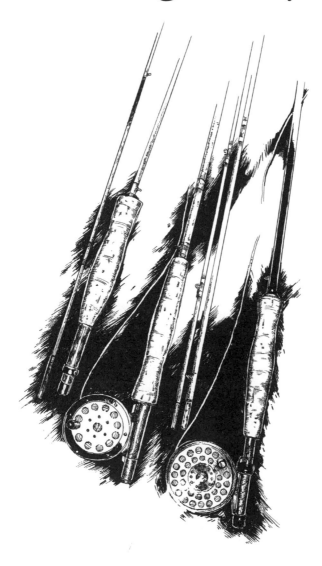

CHAPTER ONE

Rods, Reels,
Clothing, and Cameras

 FOR ME, IT HAS ALWAYS PROVEN GREAT FUN WATCHING first-time Alaska fly fishers arrive at Anchorage International Airport.

They're easy to spot, those fly fishers who've finally made it all the way to the Great Land, men and women carrying long, aluminum tubes and bags filled with fly reels and extra gear, weary and sleepy-eyed after many hours of arduous flying. The look in their eyes is one of excitement, with maybe just a pinch of wonder and a dash of jet lag thrown in for good measure.

Oh, sure, occasionally a visitor will try to make the event appear matter-of-fact, just another routine flight, just another fishing trip, just another junket on the ol' jet-setter fly-fishing agenda. Possibly. But for the most part, even those callous, world-traveled, ultra-experienced fly-fishing types find it just a little difficult not to feel like schoolkids on holiday when they first step off the plane and realize that—*finally*—they've made it to *Alyeska*. And now there is just one more leg of the journey before the final destination: the journey from Anchorage to the river—or rivers—of their dreams.

A wise fly fisher will carry his fishing gear in a tote bag over his shoulder and his rod tubes with him whenever he boards and unboards airplanes. Why carry the stuff personally? It's impossible to lose equipment if you keep it within eyesight at all times.

I'll never forget an experience at the airport at King Salmon, Alaska, a few years ago. A group of us had just arrived and were standing by an aluminum baggage chute waiting for our luggage. As we chatted, laughing and teasing one another about who was going where and who'd catch what and how big, the luggage began tumbling through the spillway.

Then, without warning, an aluminum rod tube became wedged between the baggage opening and the partition, and the rod tube buckled, forming a 90-degree angle before our eyes. As the group of us stood there gawking, to the sound of splintering graphite and bending aluminum, a two-piece fly rod was transformed into a four-piece rod—at no extra charge. We stood in shock, watching as an airline attendant raced over to remove the rod tube and straighten out the pileup. The angler standing next to me, the one with his mouth hanging open and his eyes the size of dinner plates, happened to be the owner of that rod.

Ever tried to find a fly shop out in bush Alaska where you could purchase a new, state-of-the-art graphite fly rod? Even if there was a fly shop to be found, how good might the selection be? And what would the price be this far north? Fact is, there are no sporting goods shops to be found in bush Alaska.

It was probably that very instant—that moment the rod tube buckled before my eyes—that I made up my mind once and for all. From then on, without fail, I would always hand-carry my fly rods whenever I traveled by plane.

And so I have. I've made a habit of asking the flight attendant to kindly store my rod tubes in a closet somewhere near the front of the aircraft so that I can keep an eye on them and easily retrieve them when I leave the aircraft.

When carrying two-piece rods, I usually tape a couple of aluminum rod tubes together (in opposing directions, to allow for opening from either end), not only for the sake of having an extra fly rod along—just in case—but also because fly fishing in Alaska seems to demand at least two different rod weights for the varying water conditions the fly fisher will most likely encounter. Actually, carrying two tubes in this manner is not all that bad; I've discovered that carrying two rod tubes taped together is little different from toting around one.

I also spray-paint my rod tubes different colors for quick and easy identification without having to open the tube, and I stencil my name boldly across the tubes in bright, contrasting colors. Since I've adopted that system, I've seldom had to worry about someone walking off with one of my favorite fly rods.

Many anglers find the four-piece travel rods convenient. Though they are convenient, I prefer my system of taping two rod tubes together and taking two-piece rods. I do rely on four-piece rods when traveling long distances, especially when traveling out of the United States, but I feel that the fewer joints necessary to keep a rod aligned, the better.

Fly fishers who opt for four-piece rods should carry them on board the aircraft as well, stowing them under the seat or in the overhead baggage compartment.

FLY RODS

What fly rods should a visitor take to Alaska? How many? And in what line weights?

Selecting the correct fly rod for Alaska's myriad fishing conditions and species depends as much on expected performance as on personal taste. These days, fly fishers frequently opt for rather longish, 9½- and even 10-foot fly rods. There's no doubt that the extra length of these rods makes for easier line mending and improved fly control on the water, but there are some disadvantages.

The first thing that comes to mind is portability. And we mustn't forget the disadvantages associated with landing fish, either to net or to hand, when fishing a longer rod. Shorter rods make landing a fish a much easier task. They also can create more line speed when casting, partly because there is less air resistance during the forward and rearward thrusts, and partly because shorter rods are much lighter weight and it is easier to establish tip speed—and thus faster line speed—with them.

Today, selecting a fly rod seems to be a matter of compromise, no matter how hard a fly fisher might try to make the choice a logical, scientific one.

For most of my fly-fishing situations in Alaska, I prefer light, fast-actioned, all-purpose 9-foot graphite fly rods—rods with enough backbone to handle a big fish but light enough to be enjoyable throughout a long day's fishing. For all-purpose rainbow work, I like the feel of many of the 9- and 9½-foot 5- and 6-weight rods, but for casting long, high-density sinking-tip lines, I find myself reaching for the hefting power of either a stout 7-weight or a very light 8-weight graphite rod. Usually, I select rods with fairly fast tapers, in case the winds come up and line speed suddenly becomes a factor.

But fly-rod length is relative, I've learned. Ever notice how outdoors a 9-foot rod can begin to feel more like an 8-footer, and a 10-foot rod feels more like a 9-footer? It's amazing how much longer a rod can feel inside a shop.

The extra 6 inches of a 9½-foot graphite rod feels about right to me, and though I know there are advantages to using longer rods, I've yet to be converted to toting around 10-foot fly rods.

When it comes to selecting the correct rod for going after one of Alaska's five species of Pacific salmon, the weights of the flies an angler selects, not to mention the weight of a particular sinking-tip line he might wish to employ, will have profound effects on which rod the fly fisher selects for the task at hand. And it's the same when selecting a trout/char working fly rod.

More often than many of us care to admit, the fly rod we select depends upon how we feel about it and how it feels. I know it seems finicky, but I find myself shying away from many of the 7-weight fly rods I'm tempted to add to my modest collection, no matter how pretty or impressive or efficient or effective they might prove to be.

Why? Very likely because the first really expensive graphite fly rod I ever bought was a 7-weight (a handsome, state-of-the-art, 9-footer that I proudly carried all around Pike's Market in downtown Seattle the day I bought it). It turned out it did not have enough power for the heavy, weighted streamers I wanted to cast at times, or the finesse I required for dry-fly work. Therefore, for my purposes, at least, I decided that most 7-weight rods are jinxed. Reason may tell me a stout 7-weight fly rod would make an ideal all-around rod for much of Alaska's fly fishing; experience tells me I'm better off just going with a light, state-of-the-art graphite 8-weight. Often, such an 8-weight will weigh only a tenth of an ounce more than a 7-weight, so I usually find myself opting for the 8-weight.

So I quickly turned around and sold that pretty 7-weight rod (for about half of what I paid for it) and then, digging deeper into my pockets, I opted for both a 6-weight and an 8-weight. Now I had no excuses, and better yet, I had two fly rods instead of one! I've been happy with these two line weights for most of my Alaska fishing.

There are several Alaska fly rodders who do rely on 7-weight rods as their ultimate working tool. Tom Bukowski, one of the finest rainbow trout fly fishers I've ever known, preferred a state-of-the-art, graphite, 9½-foot, 4-piece, 7-weight rod for going after trophy rainbows in the 8- to 15-pound range.

But with the ultralight graphites available today, an 8-weight will do everything a 7-weight will, and then some, without feeling all that much heavier. And when it comes to lifting a fairly heavy sinking-tip fly line out of the depths, an 8-weight is often preferable to a 7-weight.

I've also come to enjoy the feel of a good, light, 9-weight fly rod for much of the Alaska salmon fishing I do these days. To my way of think-ing, a 9-weight is a true medium-weight fly rod, a rod that's definitely in a different class than an 8-weight. Generally, a 9-weight fly rod makes for a heck of a striper rod, a fine redfish rod, and a super rod for chasing wily permit. A lightweight 9-weight also makes for a dandy of a steel-head rod and is excellent for casting into stiff winds to leery bonefish. It's a fine rod for Alaska's wide variety of 12- to 20-pound salmon, espe-cially one of today's state-of-the-art graphite numbers, which only weigh about 4 ounces.

Yes, I'm aware of those experts who swear that a 7-weight is plenty of rod for typical salmon, and that even some 6-weights will serve just fine for fresh silvers and sockeyes. True, they'll all catch fish, but a 6-weight used for bright, incoming salmon will frequently snap in two, and a broken fly rod while astream in the wilds of Alaska isn't some-thing the Alaska fly fisher wants to deal with.

In the opinions of many veterans, even 9-weight rods are not the preferred tools for the taking of king salmon. There is one point that many Alaska fly fishers seem to agree on: If there is one good all-around rod for Alaska fly fishing, it would have to be a light, 3½-ounce, 9- or 9½-foot 8-weight fly rod. Although such a rod would be too much for most char and for arctic grayling, the fishing likely would still be enjoyable, and the versatility of such a rod would be difficult to challenge.

On the other hand, an 8-weight fly rod doesn't have enough heft for battling those 18- to 20-pound, ocean-fresh chums encountered in late July in Alaska, and an 8-weight rod isn't enough for most king salmon, even though several large ones are landed on 8-weights each year.

Actually, if I were to get serious about king salmon fly fishing again, I'd probably opt for one of the new, very light, stiff 10-weights. I've recently come to know several salmon fly rodders who use these. They *can* seem heavy at first, but after fishing one a bit, a fly fisher comes to appreciate a 10-weight's casting abilities, line-hoisting capabilities, and fish-fighting strength.

I used a 10-weight rod on the Alagnak a few years ago when my brand new graphite 9-weight fly rod snapped in two on the very first chum salmon I hooked, and that 10-weight performed admirably on those powerful fish. The 10-weight also has plenty of backbone for throwing heavy flies.

For lighter, dry-fly work in Alaska, where brisk winds are always a consideration, a 6-weight rod is what many fly fishers consider to be the standard working fly rod. Many experienced Alaska fly fishers agree that a good, everyday, working trout tool for the forty-ninth state is a 9- or 9½-foot, graphite 6-weight. By employing a 6-weight rod for general work, a fly fisher can enjoy myriad Alaska fishing situations including nymphing for low-lying char on stream bottoms; swinging a wet fly through riffles, employing the intermediate technique; or carefully drifting a dry fly across pocket water with enough finesse to still enjoy the fishing. Also, many 6-weight fly rods have enough backbone to throw fairly large flies when needed, and sometimes even an occasional split shot or two, better than the 5-weights.

For dry-fly fishing, however, I've come to prefer 4-weight fly rods. Four-weights barely qualify as being wet-fly rods, but they are so pleasurable to handle and cast that it's easy for a fly fisher to rationalize and make do with one. A 4-weight makes a great rod for fishing shallow water as well as for light nymphing, and a superb rod for fluttering a dry fly to a glassy surface. I wouldn't think of climbing aboard an airplane bound for Dillingham, King Salmon, or Iliamna country without toting at least one 4-weight rod.

G. Loomis makes a dandy of a 4-weight, a rod designated as the FR1084 GLX. The *FR* stands for fly rod. The *108* indicates that the rod length is 108 inches, or 9 feet, and the *4* denotes that the rod is a 4-weight. *GLX* stands for the type of graphite used, the only graphite in existence that was designed specifically for building fly rods.

For those about to experience Alaska's fly fishing for the first time, I'd recommend taking at least three, or better yet four, fly rods (to cover all situations, and with one rod serving as backup). I recommend a 6-weight and an 8-weight (or a light 9-weight), as well as a little 4-weight for grayling and dry-fly fishing. And those who are serious about going after some large salmon should also include a 10-weight.

For general trout and char work, I recommend rigging the 6-weight with a floater, employing a long leader with a couple of split shot attached just above the surgeon's knot tied to secure the tippet. String the 8-weight with a 24-foot, 200-grain sinking-tip line, employing a big black or brown sculpin at first, and using a short 3- or 3½-foot, 10- or 12-pound leader. For the 4-weight rod, rig a weight-forward floating line (one of the new Cortland Lazer Lines or possibly a 4/5 Wulff Triangle Taper floater) with a 10- or 11-foot leader.

Cane Rods

Most people don't think of fishing bamboo when they think of fly-fishing Alaska, but there are a handful of us who wouldn't dream of

climbing aboard an airplane headed to Alaska's heartland without bringing at least one cane rod along.

Granted, my first choice for a dry-fly rod would have to be my
prized graphite 4-weight—my 9-foot GLX. But somehow, bamboo fly
rods always take me back to the innocence of the 1950s, back to when I
was still a kid, when life seemed far less pressured than it does today.

Bernie Ortman at Wood River Lodge fishes an 8-foot, Thomas &
Thomas 7-weight cane fly rod on occasion for incoming jack kings on
those beautiful rivers that run near his lodge in Alaska's Wood River–
Tikchik Lakes region. Bernie Ortman doesn't *always* fish bamboo. Like
most Alaska fly fishers, Bernie mostly relies on graphite rods.

Ted Gerken at Iliamna Lake's Iliaska Lodge has also become a bamboo aficionado. Ted finds cane excellent for grayling fishing, and he also
enjoys using a cane rod for casual char fishing from time to time.

When John Gierach joined me for his first Alaska venture a couple
of years ago, he fished nothing but a 7-foot, 9-inch, 5-weight Mike
Clark cane rod and a 9½-foot, 9-weight Jim Payne creation, a fairly
heavy yet efficient salmon rod.

On our first day of fishing, over near Lake Clark, John wanted to
catch a fresh red (or sockeye) salmon and used his Payne. He insisted that
I fish bamboo also, but instead of stringing up a Pezon & Michelle
6-weight I'd brought along, I opted for ol' Lucky, a nicely rewrapped,
recently refinished, 8½-foot, 5/6-weight Granger, my reasoning being
that the Granger, with its stout butt section, would serve well in handling
salmon, even though I was fishing for rainbows.

I still have that old Granger. It's nothing very special, just a common, all-purpose, three-piece wet-fly rod, but it's been a lucky rod for
me, and I use it every now and then just for the sheer fun of it. I even
fish it dry once in a while.

Like most fly fishers who have developed an affinity for bamboo, I've
regarded many of the cane rods I've handled as fine, handcrafted tools
specifically created for fishing flowing lines and dry flies. An angler could
risk permanently damaging a nice cane rod by casting a heavy sinking-
tip; perhaps something such as an Edwards Quadrate—an example of a
sturdy four-sided rod—might have enough backbone not to take a "set"
when casting a high density sinking-tip line, but many such rods frequently weigh upwards of 7- or 8-ounces and are unpleasant to cast.

Over the past ten years I've fooled around with several bamboo
rods. All have been fine fishing instruments, most created from six strips

of bamboo, most by notable rod makers, with some casting far superior to others. One thing is certain: Each has been unique. (One of the better casting rods, in my opinion, was an old, ugly, fast-actioned, olive and red wrapped, five sided stick fashioned some forty years ago by the late Nate Uslan.)

Len Codella, owner of Heritage Sporting Collectibles in Inverness, Florida, has said that his one, all-around favorite cane dry-fly rod is a 7-foot, 2-piece Granger 4-weight that retails for about $800 these days, but which cost well under $100 back when it was produced in the early 1950s. On the other hand Marty Keane, of Classic Rods and Tackle, Inc. in Ashley Falls, Massachusetts, has said that given an opportunity to own any bamboo rod, he'd probably opt for one of the painstakingly fashioned 5-weight creations built by either Everett Garrison or Pinky Gillum. Other bamboo aficionados swear by those rods assembled by none other than the great Jim Payne. Such rods are selling for $3,000–7,000 today.

Not many fly fishers will venture out fishing—especially to the wilds of Alaska—toting such expensive instruments. But the enthusiastic fly fisher should be aware that many of the better factory produced cane rods that were built during the fifties and early sixties (those which have received a modicum of care) are still very much around and just waiting for new owners, with many of them being entirely fishable. As this is written, the majority of them are selling for around $400 apiece.

Once you enter the world of bamboo, you can often find inexpensive cane rods that are entirely fishable. Be cautious, however, when purchasing a used bamboo fly rod, especially when purchasing one sight unseen. The snugness of fit of the old metal ferrules can be a problem area that is often overlooked. It's always preferable to have guaranteed return rights when buying previously used rods, especially when doing business long-distance.

Unlike graphite fly rods, which are all nearly identical when considering rods of the same line weight, manufactured of the same graphite, fashioned on the same mandrel, each cane rod is an individual, unique fishing instrument. A basic knowledge of the differences between common bamboo rods and rare, more valuable ones can be important when buying a rod. There is a world of difference between a Heddon factory rod, which is a fairly decent rod, and a Fred Thomas cane creation or a fine Lyle Dickerson rod, which make the Heddon seem like junk in comparison. And some bamboo rods are more appropriate for hanging above fireplaces than for being taken astream.

FLY REELS

Many fly fishers seem to feel that the more drag a fly reel has, the better. Others prefer reels without much drag. The late Mike Hershberger, one of Alaska's most renowned fly fishers, supposedly never fished Alaska with any reel having more drag than a Hardy Princess.

Certainly, there are times when a good drag on a reel comes in handy, such as the time I hooked a 13-pound char near the outlet of a stream just where it bled into a large lake. The fish was stealing all of my backing, and it finally dawned on me that maybe I'd better get my body moving downstream—and fast. In the end, I was able to recover nearly 200 yards of backing, eventually subduing that fish before carefully releasing it, all without the help of a modern drag system. Looking back on that experience, I have to admit I enjoyed battling that char without using a modern disk drag. On the other hand, I could have used a reel having a winch for a drag and ended the battle in a couple of minutes.

As far as I'm concerned, only the four largest of Alaska's five Pacific salmon species warrant using a reel with a stout drag at times. But even here, many fly fishers, including myself, believe Alaska's fishing is often at its finest when a fly fisher does not engage a high-tech drag. As Mike Hershberger used to say in his Rod and Reel fly shop in Anchorage whenever talk turned to reels with drag, "Hey, people travel all the way to Alaska to enjoy battling fish, so why would anyone want a fly reel equipped with a winch just so he can end the fight that much quicker?"

For anglers who go after 40- to 60-pound (and sometimes heavier) king salmon, however, a reel with a stout drag is required.

One day just a couple of seasons ago, I was fishing the Alagnak with Trey Combs. We were fishing for chums on floating Wogs and with pink-and-purple streamers. It was a dandy of a morning, a near-perfect, warm-weather day, and we were fishing in shallow, unbroken water with a good, steady current and plenty of room to cast. Best of all, there were plenty of fresh chums all around us—all in all, ideal conditions.

Trey and I seemed to be hooking those 13- to 18-pound chums on every other drift, several of those huge calicos taking to flight and cartwheeling upon feeling the metal, then plopping back into the currents so violently they'd send a showery spray over to the riverbank.

That's when I noticed the fly reel Trey was using. It was definitely a click reel, one of those new, jet black, jewel-like TR/3 trout reels recently introduced by Steve Abel.

"Hey, Trey, what'd you do," I shouted over, "forget your salmon outfit this morning?"

"This *is* my salmon outfit!" Trey hollered back, turning his attentions back to yet another chum chasing his fly.

Chums, much like Alaska's other Pacific salmon species (except kings), upon being hooked, often rush off in a powerful surge for 60 yards or so before returning to the main school. I'd only been teasing Trey about fishing a trout reel for salmon. That particular morning, I was trying out one of the new Penn International 2.5 reels introduced recently, even though I too have come to prefer a click reel for most of my fishing, so long as the reel is large enough to house an adequate amount of backing. In fact, most of the fishing I've enjoyed for chums and silvers over the years has been with a sturdy Hardy Marquis #8/9 click reel.

Fly fishing for Alaska's king salmon is another matter entirely. These behemoth salmon are easily Alaska's number one calling cards during June and early July, and most fly fishers use a reel fit to stop a train when fishing for *tshawytscha*. I wouldn't even consider attempting a king larger than an 18-pound jack on a reel having only a click drag although I must admit, those first couple of minutes would prove exciting!

For dry-fly fishing, the reels that have performed best for me have been my Orvis CFO III reels (for which I've acquired several extra spools, all wound and ready to pop on), with a wide assortment of line choices, or my newly acquired Abel TR/2 reels. Sometimes—when fishing for trophy-size rainbows in the 10- to 15-pound class, for example—I'll reach for one of my drag-equipped reels, either a Charlton 8400 or an Abel #1, both of which have proven to be outstanding tools, matching well with suitable rods, for any of Alaska's species.

The bottom line is that each Alaska fly fisher must decide for himself which style of fly reel is best suited for his needs for the particular species he'll be fishing.

WADERS AND CLOTHING

Although new materials are constantly being devised and tested, for many experienced Alaskans, there's still but one choice when it comes to selecting waders—neoprene. Newer, lighter, supposedly waterproof materials are constantly being experimented with, but quality neoprene waders have withstood the test of time in keeping fly fishers both dry and warm, and thus far in Alaska, nothing else has yet proven to be quite as effective in both departments.

For all intents and purposes, the days of rubber waders are all but gone. Many of Alaska's rivers are simply too deep in many places for rubber hip boots. And since neoprene waders have become very affordable and are comfortable, waterproof, and wind-resistant, they are the best all-around choice for the Alaska fly fisher.

The 3-mil thickness is best for warm-weather fishing, but for colder weather, 5-mil waders may be necessary to keep *really* warm, especially during September and October, when Alaska fishermen sometimes discover ice in their guides.

Because they offer better ankle support, I usually opt for stocking-foot neoprene waders instead of boot-foot waders. People who don't plan on being too active in their wading, though, such as elderly or handicapped fishermen, will probably be better off with boot-foot waders, which are much easier to climb into and take off. Today's boot-foot waders are also much lighter in weight than they used to be.

Having good ankle support and enjoying a good day's fishing often go hand in hand, and it's important to have a pair of top-quality wading boots. Consequently, always opt for top-of-the-line, felt-bottomed wading boots to assure steady footing, and pay the extra money to obtain the best foot support and quality possible.

Another necessity for the fly fisher is a quality fly vest with several large pockets for carrying a windbreaker, gear, flies, and assorted widgets. A long-sleeved, button-down shirt is best for most Alaska fishing situations (you can roll up the sleeves on warm days). Also take along a warm, comfortable hat, especially if you'll be fishing during the late season in Alaska. Wearing a warm hat is more important than you might think: Over 70 percent of your body heat is lost through your extremities.

Last but not least, consider the advantages of a wading belt. Theoretically, wearing a wading belt could save your life by preventing extra water from filling your waders and dragging you downstream along with the currents. In reality, however, most of today's neoprene waders fit so snugly that you couldn't get another tablespoonful of water down a pant leg if you tried. Still, a wading belt is a good safety measure, and it also adds back support, which I've come to appreciate on long days of walking and wading.

CAMERAS

Consider including a camera on your list of equipment for Alaska fly fishing. A fairly good-quality, pocket-size, water-resistant, 35mm auto-focus camera (particularly one with a built-in flash) can give you some very good photos while you're astream. You can carry such a small camera in the front pocket of your waders and you will hardly even know it's there. Although standard-size single-lens reflex cameras offer a multitude of superior lens possibilities, having a heavy SLR dangling around your neck can be awkward while fishing.

Color transparency film will give you more versatility than print film. From color transparency film, you have the options of color slides, color prints, color separations, or black-and-white prints. And slide film is often less expensive to have developed, especially if you use E6 process film, which local labs can process immediately, without having to send the film away.

Because a good percentage of the days spent astream are somewhat overcast, it is best to shoot faster films; consider using 200-speed film rather than 100-speed, or going with 100 over the tighter-grained 50-speed films. I often use the fill flash mode to add a touch of brightness to my photos.

The more you shoot photos while fishing, the more you will come to realize how difficult it is to do both well without a bit of practice. When you're astream, there's not a lot of time for obtaining quality photos, especially when catch and release remains an objective and top priority is assigned to ensuring the survival of the fish.

With a small, readily accessible autofocus camera in your pocket, you can quickly reach for the camera, open the sliding lens cover, turn the camera on, compose the shot, and quickly fire off a frame or two. It takes just a couple of seconds.

The most common error committed by photographers is not filling the frame with enough subject. The final result is a much less desirable photo of what appears to be a very small fisherman (with a large shadow over his face) displaying a very small fish. As you look through the viewfinder, tell the other fisherman the best way to position both himself and the fish.

If you are spending a day alone on a stream, you can still take photos of your catches. On several occasions, after landing a nice fish, I've reached for my autofocus camera, switched it to fill flash, filled the frame with fish and fly reel, and snapped off what have turned out to be some fairly decent photos. Better yet, if there is a shallow eddy nearby, you can lessen the possibility of any harm to the fish by allowing it to rest in the shallows for an instant while you quickly snap a picture before releasing the fish out in deeper water.

On those occasions when you catch a trophy fish, the advantages of having a camera along are obvious. Some fly fishers go to the expense of having fiberglass replicas made from photographs of trophy fish. I, however, am more than content having color enlargements made as reminders of good days spent astream.

POLARIZED SUNGLASSES

Finally, don't forget the importance of wearing sunglasses when you fish.

Polarized lenses serve two valuable functions: They take the glare off the water's surface, allowing fly fishers to see down into the water, and they protect a fly fisher's eyes from wayward or windblown backcasts. From time to time I hear stories of fly fishers hooking themselves in the eyes; I don't know about you, but that's one Alaska fly-fishing adventure I can live without!

CHAPTER TWO

Fly Lines and Leaders

 FREQUENTLY, THE SINGLE MOST OFTEN OVERLOOKED PIECE of fly-fishing equipment in Alaska—and likely one of the least understood—is the fly line.

As most anglers soon come to realize, fly lines are not all the same. Some catch fish, while others just look pretty being cast all day. There's a world of difference among fly lines, and each fly fisher serious about coming to Alaska owes it to himself to understand these differences.

There are two main categories of fly lines: *floating* and *sinking-tip*. There also are several different *tapers* of floating lines available, and seemingly as many variations of sinking and sinking-tip line configurations. The most important decision for the Alaska fly fisher, however, is when to go with a floater and when to select a sinking-tip.

FLOATING LINES

A floating line is extremely pleasant to cast, and an angler can enjoy casting all day long. A floating fly line also permits you to observe the line through every ripple and chop on the water's surface. High-visibility colored fly lines allow you to see when to mend or straighten your fly line in varying currents. It is always easier to pick up a floater off the water and make a backcast than with a sinking-tip line, which has to be hefted from the depths at which it was last drifting.

It usually doesn't matter what color a floating line is; the theory is that from the fish's point of view, all lines appear as black silhouettes. Nevertheless, since fish have been known to see fly lines zipping above them in the air and thus become frightened, suddenly darting away, you might want to be cautious about too much false casting.

Many beginners think that using a floating line means fishing at or near the surface. This seemingly logical thinking is not entirely correct, however. Floating line may also be fished deep, requiring only a long leader and some added weight to get a fly down near the bottom of the stream. In fly fishing, this technique is broadly referred to as *nymphing* (a fairly modern term that indicates fishing a nymph, or a wet-fly pattern).

In Alaska, nymphing is frequently one of the most effective methods of fly fishing. Typically, a nymph fisher will fasten a strike indicator near the end of the fly line, above an extra-long leader. Just where the tippet section is knotted on, he'll place one or two split shot (or lead wraps) of adequate size, called twist-ons. Depending on the depth of the water being fished, a weighted fly may also be helpful in achieving the correct depth. After making his final presentation, as the wet fly begins to sink and starts its underwater drift, the angler watches the strike indicator for any sudden movements or quirks (unnatural movements). Any unnatural movement of a strike indicator generally signals the presence of a fish that either has become hooked or is bumping the fly. When the angler sees such a movement, he simply raises his rod tip, or strikes, and with luck he'll set the hook.

The art of fishing just under the surface, referred to as the intermediate, or damp-fly, technique, originated back when silk fly lines would half float and half sink 6 to 12 inches under the surface. This technique is still frequently associated with Atlantic salmon fishing.

Floating lines are also used for dry-fly fishing, in which the fly floats on the water's surface and hence remains "dry."

Many of today's floating fly lines are quite impressive. I like the casting and handling characteristics of Cortland's new Lazer Line, a weight-forward number that shoots and handles well. Over the last four or five seasons, I've also come to appreciate the wonderful roll-casting characteristics and the overall versatility of the Wulff series of Triangle Taper floaters. The Scientific Anglers Mastery Series lines are also superb performers, easily some of the finest shooting lines yet devised.

If you purchase a new floating fly line for Alaska, go with a weight-forward design rather than a double taper. The need for delicate presentation in the forty-ninth state isn't quite what it might be in New York or Pennsylvania.

SINKING-TIP LINES

The tip section of a sinking-tip fly line is substantially heavier than the long, light, floating running-line portion. This can give beginners the odd feeling that the line has a hinge where the weights change. Compared with floating lines, sinking-tip lines also require more effort to retrieve before you begin another presentation. In my opinion, sinking-tip lines aren't as enjoyable to cast as floating lines. As many Alaska fly fishers discover, though, it's often the sinking-tip fly line that produces the largest fish and the greatest number of large fish.

One of the most common errors committed by newcomers to Alaska is employing the wrong fly line in the right water. I don't know how many fly-fishing magazine articles I've read where first-timers have realized a little too late that for the past week they've been fishing the wrong fly line for the task at hand. Unquestionably, the biggest reason for not catching fish is much more the choice of fly line than the choice of fly.

Determining which fly line to use in Alaska under different conditions can seem difficult at first. For example, which fly line should a newcomer going after sockeye salmon select?

This is largely determined by the water depth the fly fisher will be facing. Pacific salmon are usually encountered in fairly deep water, but this doesn't necessarily mean you should always go with an extra-high-density sinking-tip fly line when fishing for salmon. It may seem logical to use a sinking-tip fly line in water that is deeper than knee-deep, but personal preference for means of presentation still comes into play. If you feel better, and more confident, fishing a floating line rigged with lead twist-ons and a weighted fly, then by all means do so.

For Alaska fishing, a 200-grain, 24-foot sinking-tip line, such as one manufactured by Teeny, McKenzie, or Cortland, would be a good place to start. Lately, many fly fishers are opting for mini-tip sinking-tip lines, but I've had such success with 24-foot lines that I've yet to cast my first mini-tip.

Generally speaking, Alaska's Pacific salmon tend to hug stream bottoms. Often, incoming salmon are in some of the deepest waters facing the fly fisher. Some anglers don't realize this and end up drifting flies (or lures) *over* the salmon all day long, not quite comprehending why the other guy is catching all the fish. Keep in mind that when fishing for salmon, it's good to start down on a stream bottom.

In order to do this correctly, you need to have a basic understanding of the various densities of sinking-tip fly lines. A type III sinking-tip fly line doesn't sink as quickly as a type IV line, and a type IV doesn't sink as quickly as a type V (which sinks about 6½ inches per second.)

Each fly-line manufacturer has its own method for numbering fly lines, and each is seemingly always coming out with "improvements" (some better than others). But basically speaking, sinking-tip lines are manufactured to sink either moderately or quickly, and in Alaska, nine times out of ten, the wet-fly fisher will need a fast-sinking sinking-tip line.

When fishing for salmon, you usually need to get your fly down quickly, especially in heavy, deeper currents. But not always. Some swift-moving flows, such as many places along the upper Kenai, aren't as productive for a fly angler fishing a sinking-tip line as they are when he fishes a floater and a long, weighted leader. The critical thing to look for is current speed. The bottom line? If you want to fish a sinking-tip line and you think you can get your fly to the bottom sooner than halfway through a drift, you probably can. In all other situations, using a floating line with heavily weighted fly and leader is probably your best bet for reaching the bottom and maintaining a natural drift.

Some of the most productive sinking-tip fly lines for fly-fishing Alaska are the Teeny series of 24-foot sinking-tip fly lines, which are available in T-130, T-200, T-300, T-400, and T-500 designations. The *T* stands for Teeny (Jim Teeny, the designer) and the numbers indicate the weight in grains of the sinking-tip portions of the lines. There are some trade-offs here: Although a heavier line sinks faster and gets a fly down quicker, it requires a much stouter rod to throw it than does a lighter one.

In Alaska, it's not always all that easy to be fully prepared for the water conditions you can encounter in a day's fishing. One evening last season, a companion and I were returning to the lodge with our guide after a day of rainbow fishing, when we suddenly came across a school of mint-bright, incoming sockeyes.

It all seemed simple enough. All we had to do was pull over, stop the engine, get out of the boat and wade over, tie on a fly, use a 3½-foot leader of adequate strength, execute a fairly routine cast upstream of the migrating salmon, and allow our flies to sink and swing into the school of incoming sockeyes. Sounds simple enough, right?

The only problem was, I had a 300-grain sinking-tip fly line on my reel. Consequently, my casts were swinging directly *under* the incoming sockeyes, while my companion, who was fishing a 200-grain sinking-tip, was busy hooking fish on what seemed like every other cast. Here I'd purchased a brand new reel, thrown in even more hard-earned dollars for a brand new 300-grain sinking-tip line, and I couldn't buy myself a fish! I learned some valuable lessons that evening: Be prepared with a variety of alternative fly lines on extra spools, and spend the three or four minutes it takes to change spools when necessary; or when going with only one 24-foot, sinking-tip line for Alaska, make it a 200-grainer.

Many experienced Alaska fly fishers feel that the 200-grain is undoubtedly the one all-around best choice of sinking-tip fly lines for Alaska. In fact, a 200-grain sinking-tip fly line is adequate for about 80 percent of Alaska's salmon, char, and rainbow trout wet-fly situations. A 300-grain sinking-tip line has its advantages when fishing very deep-water conditions, and there are few, somewhat limited uses for a 400-grain (when fishing for king salmon, for example, which are frequently in extremely deep lies).

There are several other modern sinking-tip line variations, created by a variety of manufacturers, that you might also want to consider for Alaska fly fishing. These are 5-, 10-, and 13-foot sinking-tip lines. The only problem is, many of these frequently require additional mending to avoid bellying throughout a drift.

McKenzie also manufactures a fine series of integral shooting-head, sinking-tip lines. These are similar to Teeny's but with 25-foot integral shooting heads. Cortland, another good series, offers 225-grain sinking-tip lines.

SELECTING LEADERS AND TIPPETS
Nymphing with a Floating Line
A floating line with a long, weighted 12- or 14-foot leader and a 4X (6.0-pound) or a 3X (8.2-pound) tippet is one of the most commonly used rigs for presenting single-egg patterns to Alaska's rainbows, Dolly Varden, and arctic char. Until newer, stronger tippet materials become available, many Alaska fly fishers consider 4X to be the working tippet diameter that can be relied upon regularly for holding typical fish. As the size of the fish increases, and especially when currents are strong, the strength of the tippet must increase in proportion to the potential strain.

Fortunately, because of the vast size of the Great Land and the relatively small numbers of anglers fishing its waters, Alaska's fish generally are not as "leader shy" as many of the fish in the Lower 48. But this doesn't mean you can just go ahead and tie on a 1X tippet anytime you feel like it and experience regular hookups. As one of my first guides told me, in Alaska a fly fisher is usually best off starting with one tippet size larger than he thinks he needs, increasing the diameter of the tippet another size only if the first tippet doesn't prove strong enough. This theory has worked well for me over the seasons.

Under many typical Alaska nymphing situations, either a 4X or a

3X tippet is a good place to begin. Those times when you want to enjoy the pleasures of fishing a floating line and a long leader with a weighted fly, such as when fishing to large numbers of migrating silvers, chums, or sockeyes in shallow water, it's better to begin with a 1X (12-pound) tippet, but be ready to retie to 0X (15-pound) if necessary. Pink salmon can frequently be handled on 3X tippet material, although in swifter currents, 2X can be preferable.

Many fly fishers are astounded at discovering the strength of Alaska's Pacific salmon; be sure to approach the fishing with a selection of tippets to cover the spectrum. Also be sure to buy a reliable brand of tippet material, such as Maxima, which has earned a credible reputation in Alaska's waters for both strength and abrasion resistance.

Dry-Fly Leaders

There may be times in Alaska when you'll encounter finicky fish and will need to resort to 5X tippet material—when dry-fly fishing for arctic grayling and rainbows, for example—but such occasions are the exception rather than the rule. Hook a 6- or 7-pound rainbow in swift currents with a 5X tippet, however, and you'll quickly learn you've made a mistake. Even a good-size arctic grayling in fast currents can test the durability of many of today's 5X materials beyond their limits. Consequently, Alaska dry-fly fishers often rely on .007-inch, 4X tippet material for starters, and increase the tippet diameter as needed. If you can get away with it, 3X is a safer overall bet, but I've found that this can be pushing the visibility limit in many dry-fly situations.

Leaders for Sinking-Tip Fly Lines

One of the biggest mistakes Alaska fly fishers often make when fishing a sinking-tip line is using too long a leader. This results in the fly buoying in the currents far above the intended fishing zone. On the other hand, if a sinking-tip leader is too short, fish may be spooked by the sight of the fly line.

A 3½- to 4-foot leader is best in many cases. Whether you're fishing for trophy rainbows with a big, bulky sculpin in swift, deep currents or searching for incoming sockeyes with a sparsely tied nymph or streamer, the use of a high-density sinking-tip line is maximized when the leader is 3½ to 4 feet.

When using sinking-tip lines and 3½- to 4-foot leaders, tapered leaders are not essential, and anglers who fork out dollars for short, expensive tapered leaders are only wasting money. The practical solution is to purchase large spools of 10-, 12-, and 15-pound monofilament leader material. This will supply enough tippet material for a lifetime of service. Many serious Alaska fly fishers carry large spools of varying diameters of monofilament packed away somewhere in the pockets of their fishing vests. Securing a 3½- to 4-foot length of untapered mono using a nail knot at the end of a sinking-tip fly line is not only economical, but also effective. I prefer the wet-fly leader materials manufactured by Maxima, although there are several other excellent tippet materials on the market.

Standards for Selecting Tippets

The following are suggested beginning and standard tippet sizes for fly-fishing Alaska's sportfish species.

Species	Beginning Tippet Size	Standard Tippet Size
Arctic grayling	5X	4X
Dolly Varden	4X	3X
Arctic char	4X	3X
Cutthroat	5X	4X
Rainbows to 5 lbs.	4X	3X
Trophy rainbows	3X	1X
Pink salmon	3X	2X
Sockeye salmon	1X	0X
Silver salmon	1X	0X
Chum salmon	1X	0X
King salmon	0X	20-lb.
Pike	20-lb.	braided steel

CHAPTER THREE

Fly Patterns for Alaska

 WHEN I FIRST TOOK UP FLY FISHING IN ALASKA SERIOUSLY, like many beginners, I thought I had to have at least two hundred different fly patterns of various colors and sizes with me at all times just to begin to negotiate the maze of angling challenges that lay ahead. As the months progressed, I began to realize I was toting around some twelve or thirteen fly boxes in all, as well as a couple of Ziploc bags full of flies—most of which I never reached for. Then one day I caught my reflection in a mirror after a long day's fishing. With all the flies I had stuffed in my pockets, I looked as if I'd gained 60 pounds!

That's when it occurred to me: I was carrying around far too many flies. Worse, I didn't have the slightest clue as to when to reach for the majority of them. Sure, I was having fun with my fishing, and yes, I found myself catching a few more fish each time I went out, but only one thing remained certain: With all the flies I was carrying around, I was prepared for *any* possible Alaska fly-fishing situation.

Finally someone hinted that I'd probably do well to decide what species I was fishing for, as well as learning a little more about Alaska's sockeye salmon cycle, to begin to understand what makes Alaska's rainbows, grayling, and char behave the way the do *when* they do.

I began to inquire about the impact of the various salmon species on Alaska's indigenous fish every chance I got. What I eventually learned was that most of the people who fly-fish Alaska don't fully understand the significance of the arrival of Alaska's five species of Pacific salmon. But fly fishers should know about the important role salmon play when

26

they return to Alaska's freshwater rivers and streams in summer. By the Fourth of July, the time the sockeyes arrive, Alaska's trout, grayling, and char fishing change dramatically.

For one thing, with the arrival of the salmon, the places rainbows, grayling, and char usually are found no longer always hold fish. It's simple, really: The freshly arriving schools of salmon scare the living daylights out of Alaska's indigenous species for a time. When the salmon arrive on the scene, Alaska's rainbows, grayling, and char frequently flee from their usual haunts for a week to ten days and are seemingly nowhere to be found.

During spring and early summer, or at least until the salmon begin to arrive, Alaska's rainbows, grayling, and char survive mostly on nymphs, scuds, leeches, and sculpins as sources of nutrients. Every so often an old, rotted, bleached-out piece of salmon flesh might flush downstream (decaying salmon flesh is one of the most important nutrients for Alaska's indigenous fish), but for the most part, for Alaska's resident species, surviving another long, cold Alaska winter depends largely upon many of the bottom-dwelling fish, nymphs, and scuds for food.

It's also important for fly fishers to learn about trout and salmon fry. In late May and early June, when Alaska's streams and rivers warm up sufficiently, trout and salmon fry begin their annual downstream migrations.

Several times during early-season jaunts, my companions and I noticed what appeared to be some sort of hatch occurring at the surface. Each time I saw this, I'd immediately tie on and cast a small dry fly, fishing to the rainbows or char that were feeding in a frenzy at the surface. But my efforts always proved to be of little or no avail. I even resorted to tying up some special size 22 midge patterns, but those tiny patterns didn't work either.

Finally, one spring day, Wayne Hansen, head guide at Katmai land's Kulik Lodge, showed me a nifty Little Fry pattern he'd worked up. (He swore me to secrecy about the ingredients, but the pattern was similar to a common Fry Fly.) "The Little Fry really gets 'em excited and biting," Wayne told me. Little did he know he was giving me one of the most important Alaska fly-fishing lessons of my life.

Wayne's Little Fry made for miraculous fishing. As quickly as my companion and I could knot them on, it seemed, we'd hook another rainbow. Eventually, we took several rainbows in the 22- to 24-inch category, not exactly trophies, but big enough to raise eyebrows. Finally I was learning how to approach Alaska fly fishing during the early part of the season—the part of summer in Alaska typically referred to as spring—the time of the year when rainbows and char survive on smaller fish, be they bottom dwellers, smolt, or fry.

I began to realize that those rainbows and char I'd seen in feeding frenzies at the surface during those earlier spring outings had been feeding on tiny fry just under the surface—not on drys. No wonder those fish had refused our tiny floating dry-fly offerings!

With the arrival of the sockeyes come early July, everything changes yet again. All of a sudden hundreds of thousands of uninvited guests begin invading Alaska's freshwater rivers and streams, and dry-fly fishing seems to all but disappear for a time.

This period of transition, as it's sometimes referred to, continues throughout the Alaska summer as hundreds of thousands of salmon arrive on the scene. Then, beginning in late July and early August, hundreds of thousands of loose, drifting salmon eggs appear heading downstream, awash in the currents, providing Alaska's indigenous fish species with yet another food source.

Beginning in about mid-August in Alaska, a variety of effective fishing methods are available to the fly fisher. First, you can fish a single-egg pattern, utilizing a long leader and a floating line. Large, bushy leech patterns, such as the Egg-Sucking Leech or a big, gaudy, size 2 black-and-purple black leech, can be all but miraculous in attracting big rainbows to strike. Also attractive are a variety of White Zonker patterns: large, long, lightly colored wet flies that can be described to simulate either smolt patterns or loose, drifting, decaying salmon flesh. Flesh Flies tied in ivory-and-tan rabbit fur, perhaps with hints of subtle orange rabbit strips, can also be effective in attracting strikes during August, since rainbows at this time of the year depend largely upon decaying salmon flesh. What surprised me most, however, was how effective sculpin patterns can be during the fall, be they black, brown, tan, or olive.

Then one day it all seemed to click, and I realized that finally I was beginning to understand the Alaska sockeye salmon cycle. It's more than just the sockeyes, of course—there are four other Pacific salmon species that enter Alaska's waters annually—but beginning with the sockeyes, which arrive in great numbers, Alaska's entire freshwater cycle is disrupted, and the indigenous fish are now offered a variety of food sources.

It is also interesting to note that not all members of one fish species behave in unison. For example, recently, during the first week of September, most of the trophy rainbows we were seeking had vacated their usual holding waters and followed the various salmon species upstream to feed upon the steady stream of loose, drifting salmon eggs. But fortunately for us, not *all* of the rainbows had traveled upstream. Interestingly, territorial instincts seemed to dictate that a certain percentage of the rainbows remained near their typical haunts, seemingly guarding and protecting their favorite riffles and confluences.

Char are a different matter entirely, however. These fish can prove to be nearly as migratory as salmon. They can suddenly appear for a couple of weeks and be present in substantial numbers, only to disappear just as suddenly, following the migrating salmon or backing off into lakes.

The entire matter of the presence—or lack thereof—and predictability of Alaska's indigenous species revolves around a very real thing called *survival*. And this is why Alaska's rainbows, char, and grayling behave the way they do. Opportunists and predators that they are, especially considering the short window of time they have to take in nutrients each summer season, these fish cannot afford to pass up any opportunity at food consumption. Alaska is not like Lower 48 fisheries, where fish can be more selective, where they can savor those long, drawn-out Indian summer days and warm, extended autumns.

Yes, the Alaska fly fisher will find times when grayling and rainbows are feeding aggressively at the surface, and he will also see days when little or no surface activity seems to be taking place. There will be days when single-eggs are easily the fly of choice. But all things considered, any number of likely fly patterns are apt to induce Alaska's indigenous fish to strike.

How an Alaska fly fisher determines what fly to fish and how to go about fishing it is largely determined by the time of year. Fly fishing in Alaska really boils down to four distinct seasons: that portion of the year *before* the salmon arrive in fresh water; the period of the summer when salmon arrive; the period when the salmon are spawning and dying off; and that portion of the season after the salmon have died off and the majority of the drifting eggs and decaying salmon have washed downstream.

This is why numbers of complex, intricately tied fly patterns aren't necessary for fly-fishing Alaska. For fishing success, all the Alaska fly fisher needs is an adequate overall knowledge of the species and their basic feeding habits at different times of the season, along with a dozen or so assorted flies that will adequately represent the appropriate food items at any given time.

To help you get started, listed below are what I call my "Dirty

Dozen" Alaska patterns (a dozen basic *groups* of patterns)—flies that, year in and year out, have proven to do an outstanding job of catching fish in Alaska from mid-May through late October, including every species from arctic grayling to king salmon.

Certainly, there are other patterns, such as Mosquitoes, Hendricksons, Hornbergs, Adamses, Blue-Winged Olives, and any number of other classic wet or dry flies, that will also successfully take fish in Alaska, but once you begin to understand the life cycle and habits of Alaska's species, this basic Alaska fly selection will make sense. The flies listed here are the patterns that have proven to be the most effective for myself and for the majority of other experienced Alaska fly fishers I've come to know over the years. For the sake of practicality, let's begin our fishing on June 8— approximately three weeks after ice-out, immediately after the rainbows' annual spawning event, and the opening day of Alaska's rainbow trout season.

1. FRY (ALEVIN) AND SMOLT PATTERNS

If I had to choose just one surface pattern to fish during June in Alaska, it would be a fry pattern called Thundercreek, although a size 10 or size 8, very sparsely tied Black-Nosed Dace would probably do nearly as well, as would a Fry Fly, Fry Baby, or small Egg Smolt (a true alevin pattern— a simple surface tying with a few turns of flame chenille tied in at the head, along with a sparse green-and-white Krystal Flash wing tied in to emulate a fry's tiny body).

As a surface-fishing enthusiast, I like to either skate these small fry patterns across the surface or fish them just below. It took me a while to learn to fish these patterns properly, and I have Mike Gorton, at Goodnews River Lodge, to thank for teaching me the simplicity of fry fishing and putting the finishing touches on my presentations.

The key, he said, is to fish the fly broadside, across the currents, in order to make a fry pattern stand out among the hundreds of thousands of *real* descending trout and salmon fry and become obvious to holding fish. To do this, cast directly across stream, using a floating line and an unweighted fry pattern, forming a big, intentional downstream loop and allowing that loop to drift as far downstream as possible with the currents. Then, suddenly stop the drift by tugging the line with your line hand, at the same time moving the rod tip horizontally upstream in a low, long, deliberate movement. This helps to skate the fly, forcing the fry imitation to scurry directly across stream on the surface. Any holding trout or char will notice this sudden broadside movement, and one or more fish likely will hurry over to investigate this seemingly wounded fry as being easy prey.

2. SCULPINS, LEECHES, AND WOOLLY BUGGERS

During June in Alaska, fry descend in spurts, and you won't always find yourself standing amid a discernible fry migration. Sometimes you'll face spring water conditions where you won't be completely certain which fly pattern to try or when the next fry surge might occur. There's one key point to keep in mind: When fish are not feeding at the surface, you need to go down after them. This means using a sinking-tip line in many cases, and no flies are more visible to Alaska's resident fish than many of the big, bulky sculpin, leech, and bugger patterns.

On the Alagnak River in the northern reaches of Katmai National Park, sculpins and leeches are a must. The Alagnak is usually big water during spring and early summer of the year, and even though it's definitely fry time, frequently there are intervals when no fry seem to be present. There are no salmon entering the river in early June, so you want a fly that will prove effective in taking the resident rainbows.

Often the best solution is to tumble a big, bulky, weighted leech, sculpin, or bugger pattern downstream with the currents, using a high-density sinking-tip fly line. I simply wouldn't consider going astream during June without a good assortment of big, gaudy sculpin patterns. And foremost in my selection, along with a variety of blacks, browns, and olives, would be several large, size 2, light brown and dark brown mink-tied numbers, a specialty tying that Tom Haugen, head guide at Katmai Lodge, showed me.

For fishing these patterns in fairly deep-water situations, a high-density, 24-foot sinking-tip line is best. Often, merely dangling a big, ugly sculpin, leech, or bugger pattern at the lower reaches of a seam or confluence will surprise a fly fisher with a sudden, line-jarring strike. This technique, sometimes referred to as "fishing a hangdown," can be extremely effective. Some of these takes by hungry trophy rainbows are so sudden and powerful that a fly fisher—especially one standing in waist-high or deeper currents—must keep a firm grip on his rod and plant his feet securely.

There are conflicting theories regarding the presentation of large, weighted flies, however. One school of thought is that the fly should always be fished straight downstream, *with* the currents. Other fishers maintain that allowing a sinking-tip line to sweep a fly across a stream bottom in a long, swinging arc—*across* the currents—draws more attention to what the fish perceive as an escaping meal. I like to combine the two techniques, doing both on each drift.

To fish these flies, cast slightly upstream across the current, allowing the fly to sink, and begin drifting. Then, after making one big upstream mend, as the fly begins to swing in the currents (coming near the end of its arc), hold on tight and be ready for a strike, because some of the strongest takes come at this time (known in fly fishers' jargon as "on the swing"). One or two fish frequently will start to follow the "escaping" fly as it drifts past them, when suddenly one of them will strike—hard— just at the turn. Why? It is believed that at this moment, as the fly speeds up in the currents, the fish decides its prey is starting to get away from it and its aggressive instincts take over.

If no take occurs at this point, keep letting out fly line, allowing the fly to continue tumbling in the currents far downstream, down to where the fly appears to have reached another confluence, and there you should begin yet another hangdown. You may discover at this point that you're getting deep into your backing.

An important key to fishing sinking-tip lines is to impart a bit of life to the fly, adding motion either by wiggling the rod tip or by moving your arm from left to right, then back again, thus sliding the fly sideways in the currents.

Good flies for these deep, wet-fly situations include the always effective standard Woolly Bugger series (purple, black, brown, and olive are the commonly used colors), including such excellent dressings as the Electric Woolly Bugger. This is tied in the same manner as a standard Woolly Bugger, with a few strips of Krystal Flash added along the sides of the fly, extending down into the undulating, marabou tail. Over the seasons, an olive Electric Woolly Bugger has proven to be one of my favorite flies for fishing big, muscular arctic char and sea-run Dollies.

Another effective fly, the Strip Leech Fly, is created from long, thin strips of black, purple, or brown rabbit fur. These flies are often 4 to 5 inches long, like the real Alaskan leeches. These thin Strip Leech Flies usually are tied on a hook that has been severed in the middle of the shank. The front half is connected to the rear half, which is tied on at the tail of the fly, by braided nylon backing. Lately, some superb String Leech Flies have appeared on the scene. These strong, resilient flies are made from braided steel leader material bonded together by wrappings of stout Kevlar thread and will sink as they swirl with the currents.

Fished with either a floating or a sinking-tip line, Strip Leech Flies can be absolutely deadly on Alaska's trophy rainbows.

Egg-Sucking Leeches are commonly fished—very effectively—for *all* of Alaska's fish species. Fished with either floating or sinking-tip lines, by dead-drifting or via a loose, tumbling motion, these purple-and-pink creations have become famous in Alaska for their ability to evoke line-jarring strikes. ESLs are most commonly tied with purple bodies and undulating, purple marabou tails, with a pink egg tied in at the head. Tied extra-large, they make one of the best patterns for taking Alaska's giant king salmon. Whether fish see ESLs as leeches or are more attracted to the egg portion is not known for certain; all scores of Alaska fly fishers know is that fish frequently attack ESLs—savagely. Consequently, purple Egg-Sucking Leeches in a variety of sizes definitely deserve an important spot in every Alaska fisher's fly box.

3. WHITE ZONKERS

I've often been amazed at the success of the White Zonker patterns. They are often deadly on large char and lake trout and seem especially effective on silver salmon. These flies seem to play a dual role. With its white rabbit-fur tail and overbody and its pearlescent Mylar underbody, a White Zonker imitates a smolt pattern rather nicely. It also fairly simulates decaying salmon flesh, even if it is a bit too white. Char frequently take these patterns with reckless abandon—as smolt, I believe—and rainbows will often come off their lies and follow such a fly, probably reacting to it initially as drifting salmon flesh.

The Sarp's Perfect, a fly devised by one of Tony Sarp's clients on the Alagnak, is a close relative to the White Zonker, except that the Sarp's has a brilliant, white, cactus-chenille body and a white rabbit-fur wing, with a flame-colored single egg tied in at the head, serving as a triple attractor.

4. FLESH FLIES AND BUNNY BUGS

Most Alaska fly fishers are aware of the effectiveness of Flesh Flies during late summer and fall in Alaska, when Ginger Bunny Bugs imitate drifting, decaying salmon flesh. But it may come as a surprise to some that Flesh Flies are also effective during the early season. Given the amount of loose, decaying salmon flesh drifting in many of Alaska's rivers during the late fall and winter, however, it shouldn't be all that surprising.

Flesh patterns also have been known to evoke leech or sculpin responses from trout, stimulating reflex actions reinforced the previous autumn. Thus the Ginger Bunny Bug, or flesh-colored Flesh Fly, may serve a dual role. These large, pulsating, rabbit-hair flies appear very life-like underwater as they drift along with the currents, especially so when they are stripped, or when intentional action is imparted.

Ironically, it was a fishing companion from Colorado who was the first to show me the effectiveness of fishing these flies. It was mid-July, on Alaska's lovely Talachulitna River, and no salmon were even close to dying or decaying at this point in the season. I wasn't in the habit of fishing flesh, relying mostly on nymphing single-egg patterns.

Tom looked through his fly box and decided on a big, bulky Ginger Bunny Bug. He tied it on the end of his 4-foot leader, which was nail-knotted to a 200-grain sinking-tip fly line. Swinging his line through a pretty riffle, Tom quickly hooked and released a 27-inch, 8-pound male and then a fine, heavily spotted, 24-inch, 6-pound hen. I had probed those very same riffles only minutes earlier with a single-egg pattern, hooking only one measly 3-pounder.

When I looked more closely at Tom's fly, I noticed that he'd tied in a couple of strips of burnt orange rabbit fur to better simulate decaying salmon flesh. Tom told me he'd experienced wonderful success fishing a Flesh Fly. He let me try one, and two casts later I hooked into a chunky 5-pound rainbow. I've been a fan of these versatile flies ever since.

Other Bunny Bugs—large cerise, orange, and chartreuse ones in sizes 1/0, 2/0, and 3/0—are some of the preferred king salmon flies in Alaska today. Sparse, small, size 6 and size 8 cerise, orange, and chartreuse Bunny Bugs also frequently work wonders in attracting pinks to strike.

5. SOCKEYE SALMON AND PINK SALMON FLIES

Small, sparsely tied flies, such as many of the more common steelhead patterns (Fall Favorite, Freight Train, and so on), often prove very effective for taking red, or sockeye, salmon. Since salmon are not in fresh water to feed, and since sockeyes are officially plankton eaters, fishing a small, colorful, sparsely dressed pattern frequently gets a fly angler into several sockeye hookups during a day's fishing. Other excellent patterns for hooking fresh bluebacks, or sockeye salmon, include a size 6 Brassie; a size 2 Pink Shrimp, a short body of pink chenille simply palmered with a white hackle; a small, lightly dressed brown, purple, or orange Krystal Bullet or Sparkle Shrimp; and a size 2 purple or flame Teeny Nymph.

Although thousands of roadside anglers fly-fish for sockeyes using inexpensive, unsophisticated, fairly long streamers called Coho Flies, many more experienced fly fishers tend to believe the key to hooking sockeyes consistently is to fish small, sparse flies. The secret is to locate sockeyes in moderately moving water and to present these small, sparsely tied flies, whether via a floating or a sinking-tip line, directly in the paths of the holding salmon.

Pink salmon are well known for striking at a variety of smaller, colorful, flashy wet flies such as size 6 and size 8 Comets, Polar Shrimps, and double-egg flies, as well as various shades of size 8 single-egg patterns. In my experience, though, nothing has attracted pink salmon more quickly than size 6 pink, cerise, and orange Mylar-bodied Sparkle Shrimp patterns.

6. PINK, PURPLE, AND ORANGE POPSICLE STREAMERS

Chum and king salmon, especially, are attracted to the gaudy pink, purple, or orange Popsicle Streamer patterns, which are frequently tied on size 2 and size 1/0 hooks. I'm not as much into king salmon fly fishing and aching elbows these days as I used to be (my right elbow is still recovering from bursitis), but I dearly love to fly-fish for chums at or very near the surface during late July and early August. I've found that mint-bright chum salmon are best fished in moderately flowing, knee-deep or shallower currents, and a fly fisher casting to a school of chums, stripping one of these brilliantly colored Popsicle Streamers, or a very similarly tied fly called a Show Girl, will frequently experience a high percentage of hookups.

7. SINGLE-EGG PATTERNS

Single-eggs are undoubtedly the most successful flies in Alaska during late summer. Even though single-egg patterns might not seem like flies at first, when you begin hooking fish you'll soon realize that fishing an egg pattern is merely the Alaska version of matching the hatch.

Two major styles of single-egg flies are commonly used in Alaska: Glo-Bugs, which are trimmed yarn flies, and Iliamna Pinkies, smaller, pink chenille-wrapped flies. Single-egg patterns are tied in myriad colors to match local, drifting egg colors, although pink, peach, apricot, and flame are the most widely used. The wide range of colors can make single-egg selection a technical one.

Single-egg flies are tied and fished to resemble loose, drifting salmon eggs. Size 10, 8, and 6 short-shanked hooks are generally used. They are best fished with a floating fly line, employing an extra-long leader, with perhaps a strike indicator attached at the junction of line and leader and one or two split shot or lead wraps attached about 12 inches above the fly, enabling the egg pattern at the point to "boondog," or drift along with the swirling currents very near the stream bottom, creating a very natural-looking drift.

Single-egg flies can be effective during the entire season, but they reach the height of their effectiveness beginning in mid-August and extending into late September. All species, including sockeyes, will readily strike at these patterns. Even king salmon are sometimes hooked on single-eggs, especially a very large pattern called a Fat Freddy.

Lately, some Alaska fly fishers have begun using plastic beads to represent single eggs. These are very effective but personally, I draw the line at fishing plastic beads.

Glo-Bugs and Iliamna Pinkie single-egg patterns are musts for fly-fishing Alaska beginning in late July. Both of these flies make excellent choices for the first-timer who simply wants to get out there and catch fish.

Serious, experienced Alaska rainbow, char, and Dolly Varden fly fishers depend on specialized shades of single-egg patterns to take large, trophy-size fish, whether fishing big, deep, fast-flowing currents similar to those found at the Kenai or smaller, remote wilderness streams where trout the size of footballs, which have followed salmon to a stream's headwaters, are sometimes found.

8. PEACOCK DRYS, BLACK ANTS, AND ELK-HAIR CADDIS DRYS

If I had to choose only one dry fly for Alaska, it would probably be one of the outstanding peacock-tied drys, such as a size 12 Griffith's Gnat, a Renegade, or a Royal Wulff. Peacock-tied flies seem to resemble all manner of juicy insects that rainbows and grayling are highly attracted to. At times I've seen rainbows become so excited at the sight of drifting peacock that they've darted to the spot just to be the first in line to intercept these buggy-looking offerings.

In Alaska, with its short seasons, sheer survival is the name of the game as far as Alaska's indigenous fish species are concerned, so matching the hatch isn't nearly as important as it is in some areas of the Lower 48. What *is* important is presenting drys properly, presenting something that appears realistic and that looks to be a hearty food source—something that looks to be a *meal*. This is where peacock comes into play. In the case of a large Griffith's Gnat, the palmered hackle adds a very lifelike appearance. A Renegade, with its opposing wings, might appear more like an ant or possibly a spider. And no list of flies for Alaska would be complete without the deservedly famed Royal Wulff. In its standard sizes, it's a dandy; when fished in larger sizes, it's a superb attractor of *big* fish.

If you'd like some exciting surface action in Alaska, try casting a size 8 or a size 6 Royal Wulff over to a good-looking piece of water, twitching it a bit, and holding on to your cork. These oversize flies can evoke sudden strikes from very large rainbows seemingly appearing out of nowhere. Remember to apply generous amounts of fly floatant to both your fly and your leader before fishing these oversize drys.

One cold winter's day a few years ago, I found myself with some time on my hands and decided to attempt to create a dry fly that would both catch fish and float without fly floatant. The result was Dan's Flying Ant, which is nothing more than a rectangle of black or red closed-cell foam tied on a hook over a squirrel-tail tail (slightly round the sharp-cut corners of foam with the coolest flame of a butane lighter) and finished with a couple of wraps of grizzly hackle over the thorax. The following season, I tried one of these foam flies and was pleased with the results. Both rainbows and grayling take them readily in size 14 or size 12.

Another essential dry fly for fly-fishing Alaska is an Elk-Hair Caddis. Alaska does have some impressive insect hatches (even on salmon rivers when salmon are present), and sometimes the sizes of these hatches are truly astounding. One warm, bright day in mid-June, a group of us were astonished by the size of a caddis hatch that occurred on the Alagnak as we were pulling up to an island for lunch. It actually looked as if it had begun snowing!

Various colors of caddis imitations are readily available to the Alaska fly fisher—everything from black to light blond, although the naturals most commonly seen floating downstream are tan and light brown. As in most other dry-fly applications in Alaska, matching the hatch isn't always essential. In several situations, I've intentionally switched to a darker or lighter color just so I could keep an eye on the fly I was fishing. And often during a caddis hatch, throwing an entirely different bug—say, a Royal Wulff, an Irresistible, or a Renegade—is about the only way you can distinguish your fly from the hundreds of drifting caddis afloat.

One afternoon, while I was fishing a remote tributary leading to a large lake down on the Alaska Peninsula, huge mayflies began appearing at the surface every few seconds. Almost as suddenly, enormous grayling began to appear. During the next couple of hours, my companions and I hooked and released more than a dozen in the 19- to 21-inch range. Which fly did we use? A large, tan Elk-Hair Caddis.

In many of Alaska's prime grayling waters, the Wood River–Tikchik Lakes region and the famed Ugashik Narrows, Elk-Hair Caddis can be amazingly effective. At the outlet of Lake Kulik—the uppermost lake in the connected Tikchik chain—I was surprised by the number of midsize grayling that hit on caddis patterns.

9. STIMULATORS AND STONEFLY SURFACE IMITATIONS

I enjoy fishing large drys, and one of the main reasons for this is a fly called the Stimulator. To me, one of the most exciting things in life is to be standing out in the currents, casting a 4-weight line with a size 6 dry fly over near a cut bank, with the anticipation that any minute now, very possibly a 10-pound rainbow will come up and grab my fly. Granted, a 10-pound fish at the surface is not an everyday occurrence—even in Alaska. But it is exciting when such a fish is taken on a dry, to say the least.

This is why I've come to love fishing oversize drys, and Stimulators, based orange, red, or chartreuse, act as marvelous attractors, as well as being an alternative to the norm.

The Stimulator is a stonefly imitation, but as Alaska's rainbows, char, and grayling are opportunistic feeders, it's not terribly important that a stonefly hatch is actually taking place when you use one. Yes, Alaska has stoneflies, and yes, the Alaska fly fisher will encounter brief stonefly hatches from time to time, but Alaska's rainbows, char, and grayling don't wait to decide whether or not there's a *real* stonefly hatch occurring; they'll usually go out of their way to grab what they can *when* they can, suddenly reacting to these tasty-looking morsels adrift at the surface.

10. FLASH FLIES AND EVERGLO FLIES

Along with the Egg-Sucking Leech, the silver Flash Fly ranks as one of my favorite choices for attracting strikes from silver—or coho—salmon. Newcomers to this silvery pattern are frequently amazed at the aggressiveness with which silvers will feverishly strike at these shiny, tinselly creations.

Commonly tied in weighted size 2 or size 4 versions, Flash Flies, with their silvery bodies and red or orange hackles over silver Flashabou tails, make for especially visible flies in many of Alaska's silty, glacially fed rivers. Everglo Flies, which glow in the dark, are usually tied in either chartreuse or orange. Many fly anglers also fish Everglo Flies with success for silvers, although the Everglo series is best known for scoring excellent marks on Alaska's big kings.

11. SURFACE PATTERNS: MICE AND SHREWS, DAHLBERG DIVERS, WAKING FLIES, AND WOGS

Fishing deer-hair and antelope-hair mouse patterns at the surface is one of my favorite methods of fly-fishing for Alaska's rainbows, and many other anglers who have tried them feel the same way. Mouse and shrew patterns make some of the most exciting rainbow fishing in Alaska. The object is to cast over near or up on the bank, and then allow the mouse to splash down into the water and squirm away, crossing the current. This is best done by waggling the rod tip and applying short, quick strips with the line hand at the same time. Size 2 and size 1/0 long-shanked hooks have proven best for creating these numbers.

And the same can be said for fishing specialty surface patterns—the Dahlberg Diver, for instance—to Alaska's northern pike. Such patterns cause great commotion at the surface and attract the attention of wily predators lurking below.

The Micro Mouse is a smaller variation of a typical deer-hair or antelope-hair mouse, with a gray foam body, 20-pound monofilament for whiskers, and a thin leather tail tied on a size 4 hook. Frans Jansen, the Alagnak guide who developed this surface pattern from ultramodern materials, has succeeded in converting many a rainbow trout enthusiast to this effective small pattern.

If you appreciate action at the surface, be sure to try some of the surface flies that are tied to cause an intentional wake there. Lani Waller's Waller Waker is probably the best known of these waking patterns, but there are several other proven patterns, such as the common Bomber and a host of other, mostly large, custom floaters. Fly anglers who learn to fish these large attractors at the surface, intentionally imparting a fluttering motion to them, causing the floating fly to wake, are often impressed with the results. Most Alaska fly fishers who try these patterns use floating lines and flutter large drys regularly, eagerly fishing the surface, always on the lookout for those dramatic "alligator wakes" as Alaska's curious—and hungry—predators close in for a meal at the surface.

Wogs, short for Polly Wogs, are large, pink or chartreuse surface patterns, tied with deer hair, and intentionally trimmed with blunt, bulbous heads. Chum and silver salmon, particularly, often attack these brightly colored surface patterns with a vengeance. The idea is to cast and then strip or skate the Wog in front of sighted fish and attract the fish's attention. (Casting these large, very wind-resistant flies is best accomplished using a stout rod.)

Eight times out of ten, upon seeing such an offering at the surface, a fresh-from-the-ocean silver will turn and suddenly strike. I don't think anyone knows for certain what salmon take Wogs to be, but the fact remains that silver salmon and chums attack them violently.

12. NYMPHS

No list of basic flies for Alaska would be complete without a couple of basic nymph patterns. During those in-between season periods, the common Gold-Ribbed Hare's Ear Nymph and a brown or black G.P. (general-purpose) Nymph can go a long way toward rounding out the Alaska fly fisher's all-around assortment.

There are times—especially before and between distinct salmon runs—when nothing seems to work. Often, at these times, I've found that simply fishing a nymph will quickly get me into fish. A common size 10 or size 8, brown Woolly Worm has proven very effective for me on several occasions, as has a small Teeny Nymph. Resorting to a big, heavy nymph, such as a Kaufmann's Giant Stonefly, frequently serves in getting a fly fisher down deep, down to where fish are holding, quickly eliciting a strike (especially in the early season). Frequently, these big, ugly, extra-heavy nymphs are in a class by themselves in getting stubborn fish—especially in spring and early summer—to suddenly come to life.

PART TWO

The Alaska Experience

CHAPTER FOUR

Bush Planes and Fly-Outs

LIKE MANY ALASKA FLY FISHERS, ESPECIALLY ON GOOD DAYS, I look forward to the flying required to get to many of the Great Land's premier fisheries nearly as much as the fishing itself. Unless the winds come up or clouds sock in an area, flying across Alaska usually proves to be a great, wondrous, scenic adventure. If the weather *does* decide to act up a bit (which can be fairly frequently), the adventure is only multiplied.

Climbing into a small bush plane and soaring up over snowcapped, glacial mountain ranges, rolling, forested countrysides, and turquoise blue lakes makes for pure, unadulterated adventure. The fact that in just a few more minutes you'll be arriving at some of North America's ultimate fishing waters only serves to enhance the excitement.

Alaska has very few roads, and a person doesn't get around very well or very far without an airplane. Those rivers and streams located on the limited highway systems often become overcrowded with drive-to anglers. In order to get to some of the best fishing, it's necessary to fly there.

Anchorage's Lake Hood, the busiest float plane base in the world, buzzes like a beehive from mid-May through late September, many of its float planes carrying anglers to otherwise inaccessible wilderness rivers and lakes. Living in Anchorage, I don't need to look outside the tell when the ice has melted; hearing the float planes roaring d tells me it's time to get out the fly rods. Sometimes I drive to Lake Hood to watch the float planes taking off and landing and e photos, standing out on a little grassy peninsula of land only feet n where the float planes buzz by.

There are several large-scale Alaska air services, including Ketchum's Air Service, on the north shore of Lake Hood, Rust's Flying Service, with its large fleet of dark red Cessna 207s, deHavilland Beavers, and Otters, and Trail Ridge Air, with its beautiful two-tone, blue Beavers.

The landing gear options for Alaska's aircraft seem endless. At various times of the year, bush planes might be equipped with small, regular tires; large, balloonlike "tundra tires"; pontoon floats; float-and-wheel combinations (amphibs); skis; or ski-and-wheel combinations. Aircraft owners and lodges determine which type of landing gear will best meet their needs at any particular time of year, depending upon the uses demanded of the aircraft, although frequently the pilots find themselves wishing they had a different kind of landing gear installed. Under emergency conditions—theoretically, at least—even a float-equipped aircraft could probably make an emergency landing on a gravel bar or on a remote plot of tundra if necessary.

Even with bush aircraft, there are some places that aren't accessible unless you're willing to make a trek on foot. Sometimes a tundra lake will not be large enough for an airplane to make a landing and subsequent takeoff. Pilots often take fly-bys for closer looks and make last-minute judgment calls based on both past experiences and quick calculations considering the gross weight of the aircraft together with the prevailing winds. Consequently, just because a fly fisher finds himself wanting to fish a particular river doesn't mean he'll be able to fish it.

Though most Alaska pilots are experienced professionals and are very competent, in the course of my travels I've come across a couple whom I should have known better than to climb in an airplane with. It's up to you to decide whether or not to fly with a particular pilot. Follow your instincts. It's not worth risking your life in this mountainous terrain for the sake of fly fishing.

CHAPTER FIVE

Weather Permitting

THERE'S A SAYING THAT GOES "IF YOU DON'T LIKE THE weather, just wait a few minutes . . . it'll change." Whoever said that was probably talking about Alaska.

If you have access to a topographical map of Alaska, take a good look at it, paying particular attention to the mountain ranges and their nearby coastal valleys. What should quickly become apparent is the disparity between the areas at sea level and where some of North America's tallest, most abrupt mountains begin. In short, many regions of Alaska get steep quickly.

Alaska often has a less-than-subtle way of reminding humans that Mother Nature is the real boss. Most professional pilots know this, and amateur pilots need to always remember it. Even the brown bears sometimes take respite from the weather and shelter under bushes until the winds quit gusting. If you've never tried casting a fly line in Alaska's stiff breezes, it'll teach you the difference between casting a 4-weight and an 8-weight in a hurry, and it'll make you glad you brought both.

But it isn't *always* windy in Alaska. Sometimes it can be spectacularly calm and clear, and you'll become caught up in Alaska's pristine wonders.

Many of the trips I've made from Anchorage through Lake Clark Pass to Iliamna country remain vivid in my memory. Pilots who regularly fly through Lake Clark Pass know it's an awe-inspiring cut of jagged mountains with huge, weathered glaciers on both sides. Maybe it's not as treacherous as flying through Merrill Pass or Rainy Pass, but don't try telling that to the families of the dearly departed who haven't made it back home for Sunday brunch over the years.

Along the valleys of Lake Clark Pass exist several wandering, ever-changing glacial streams, often appearing chalky from the glacial silt they carry on their downstream journeys. It's beautiful, rugged country, what with its meandering tributaries and many steep, glacially scarred slopes.

The first time I ever made this journey was in the backseat of my friend Tom Bukowski's Piper PA-12. PA-12s, like Super Cubs, are mostly fabric-covered airplanes, many in Alaska equipped with large, balloonlike tundra tires that usually allow pilots to land almost anywhere without getting stuck in the muck or bending the airplane. It was almost a three-hour ride, the weather was perfect, and Tom and I marveled at the scenic beauty of the glaciers and mountains peaks below.

Yet on another flight through Lake Clark Pass, things were very different. I was flying with Frank Plunk, the former owner of Big Mountain Lodge, that day, in Frank's Cessna 182, a fast, small-wheeled, single-engine airplane. Compared with flying in a Super Cub, it was like riding in a fancy limousine.

Halfway through the pass, dark, heavy, black clouds socked in and totally blocked out any view we might have enjoyed of the steep surrounding mountainsides. That's when I remembered we were flying through some of the narrowest canyons and most treacherous mountains in Alaska.

I suggested to Frank that we turn around and head back to Anchorage, but because Frank couldn't see either, he didn't dare risk attempting a turn. Our only option was to slow the airplane down, drop to a lower altitude in hopes of better visibility, and attempt to follow the glacial river below.

Then we hit turbulence, and my head bounced off the ceiling of that Cessna so hard it hurt. What *really* had me concerned, though, was not being able to catch any glimpse whatsoever of those steep, rugged mountains through the thick, gray clouds.

By the time we'd dropped to 400 feet and the clouds had begun to dissipate slightly—enough that we could begin to see splotches of gray mountainside and a few scattered spruce trees—I began to realize we would probably survive our flight through the pass. A minute later, we caught a brief glimpse of the waters of Lake Clark below us. Apparently we'd made it through.

Our fun wasn't over yet, however. Down below us, we could begin to make out huge whitecaps on what is frequently a very flat, calm, aqua blue lake. That's about the time I noticed we were flying cockeyed, a tactic pilots sometimes resort to in an attempt to keep an airplane headed in the right direction. Except for getting bounced around a lot, somehow we survived that ordeal. My head hit the ceiling a couple more times, though I tried to act like I didn't notice the turbulence.

Eventually we crossed Lake Clark and parts of huge Iliamna Lake. Our approach to the airstrip was a wild, quartering affair. Landing sideways is even more exciting than flying sideways, I discovered. We made a "hot," bouncy landing on a dirt strip the lodge owner had carved out of the tundra behind his lodge and came to a stop just shy of the lodge building, not 20 feet this side of the kitchen door.

What we experienced that day, I was assured, was considered but a routine, uncomfortable airplane flight, "routine" only in that it happens that way in Alaska sometimes—that is, whenever one is caught in inclement weather. Usually, there's little else one can do in situations like this but wait it out and hope everything turns out all right, for when a large Alaska storm system suddenly develops (many arriving by way of the Aleutian Islands), man is quickly reminded that he is but mortal and is at the full mercy of the elements.

In Alaska, you hear stories of fliers suddenly encountering wind shears and ending up in trees and *sometimes* walking away, or of people in small planes getting ditched in lakes and somehow surviving the incident, but these certainly aren't adventures any of us look forward to, even though most of us are aware that things like this can—and do—happen on occasion.

Just this past season I was talking with a lodge pilot who told me of a recent afternoon when he was nearly dozing in his airplane, waiting for a group of clients to complete an afternoon's fishing, when he looked up and saw a deHavilland Beaver (with five people aboard, he later discovered) suddenly catch a wind shear and ditch nose-first in the nearby lake. He started the engine and quickly taxied over to where the Beaver went down. He rescued the passengers and pilot and hurried them back over to the beach. "Luckily," he said, "I was able to reach them in time before they drowned or hypothermia could set in."

But life-and-death situations aren't the only adventures that can cause a person to develop a respect for Alaska's weather. Sometimes just a dash of the forty-ninth state's chilly breezes can cause a person to reflect on the necessity of toting adequate clothing.

A few years ago, I was on a late-September fly-fishing junket in Iliamna country when the thermometer suddenly dipped. The first two days of that trip it was Indian summer, but then overnight, ice began forming at the river's edges, not to mention on our fly lines and in our rods' guides.

Being out there in late September wearing nothing but shirtsleeves seemed no big deal at first, but when I found myself spending half of my fishing time just trying to survive the cold and attempting to move my frozen fingers and wiggle my toes, I began to realize the importance of wearing sufficiently warm clothing. Just because I wanted an endless Alaska summer didn't mean I was going to get it. I did manage to borrow a hat and sweater from a visitor from California. I learned a very good lesson on that trip about always taking along proper clothing.

Probably the best advice for Alaska's visiting anglers regarding its unpredictable weather is to bring along adequate clothing, and don't be too rigid in expecting to keep to return schedules; Alaska's occasional inclement weather might just keep you grounded for a couple of days longer than you originally planned. Also, if something tells you not to board a boat or an airplane, don't do it. Stay in the tent or back at the lodge and practice dominoes. After all, if the brown bears aren't braving the elements, why should you?

It's called "weather permitting" in Alaska, and granted, for many first-timers, any delays affecting travel schedules might seem a bit irritating. After a second or third visit to the Great Land, however, and after you've enjoyed the thrills of catching and releasing Alaska's trophy fish, experiencing inclement weather now and then while spending time at an Alaska fishing lodge will be something you find yourself looking forward to.

CHAPTER SIX

Alaska's Fishing Lodges

OVER THE PAST DECADE, AS AN OUTDOOR WRITER AND photographer, I've had the opportunity to visit and experience some twenty-five of Alaska's finest and less-than-finest fishing lodges. Some of them definitely qualify as being "premier," while others only bill themselves as such. All have been fun places to visit. I've learned, however, that "premier" means different things to different people. To me, a premier lodge has warm running water, offers me a private room (no matter how unsophisticated), provides good fishing, serves Diet Pepsi, and lets me sleep in every once in a while.

Each of Alaska's fishing lodges is different, and each has its own pluses and minuses. Many are wonderful places where the fishing is great and a visitor ends up making lifelong friends. If you revisit the same lodge year after year, you know what you'll be in for, but you can never know for a certainty just what you might discover elsewhere, no matter how many hours you spend researching brochures beforehand. On several occasions I've spent hours attempting to ascertain the flavor of a lodge sight unseen, but nine times out of ten, when I finally arrive at the place, I'm surprised by something or other.

The personalities you encounter can help determine the quality of your experience almost as much as the lodge's setting or ambience. On one occasion, I couldn't wait to get away from a lodge. The head guide there was a slothful, obnoxious braggart who knew *everything* there was to know about fishing—and hunting for that matter—and wouldn't let a single comment or conversation go unheralded.

Another time (although this was not a typical situation), I was thrown in with five guys who never quit drinking, it seemed, and who wouldn't quit talking (yelling was more like it) until way into the wee hours, long after I was getting droopy-eyed and wanted to call it quits for the night, even though I'm usually one of the last to turn in. To top things off, three of them snored proficiently, so I'd have to beat them to sleep or I might as well get up and get dressed and go out into the main lodge and tie flies all night. Their only saving grace was that all five of them were exceptional fly fishers who had obviously spent a fair amount of time practicing their craft. Lesson learned: Bring a good companion for that "trip of a lifetime."

Where a lodge exists plays an important part in the overall experience as well. For example, it's always nice to be able to go out after dinner and get in another hour or two of fishing. Fly-out lodges must rely on decent weather to get their clients out to the fishing, just as they have to rely on generous amounts of camaraderie and entertainment to keep their clients occupied on cloudy, windy days. This isn't all bad, mind you, but it isn't as nice as being able to step outside to the river every once in a while to wet a line.

I'm frequently amazed at how well most lodges can make guests feel at home. Most have delivered more than I expected, not only in terms of comfort, but also in numbers and sizes of fish.

A week's stay at an Alaska fishing lodge costs anywhere between $1,500 and $6,000. The price doesn't always reflect the actual quality of the place; I know of one $1,500 lodge that is every bit as good as some of the $5,000 lodges I've stayed at. However, the average cost of a quality Alaska fishing lodge is $3,000 to $3,750 per week, or $500 to $600 per day, gratuities not included. This may sound like a lot of money, but it includes deluxe shelter, gourmet meals, express room service, fishing instruction, fly-tying bench and materials, flies, fly changes, and professional guides and float plane pilots, not to mention boats and float planes.

CHAPTER SEVEN

Alaska's Bears

 SOONER OR LATER, WHETHER YOU WANT TO OR NOT, IT'S almost inevitable that you'll encounter one of Alaska's brown bears *(Ursus arctos)* while fly-fishing, particularly in the wild coastal regions officially designated as being anywhere within 75 miles of the coast.

Alaska's fishing bears are not black bears, those smaller, "park bears" found in places like Yellowstone. Alaska's brown bears are grizzlies, the world's largest bears. Some of these bears, also known as Kodiak bears, have reached lengths of nearly 10 feet, and several weighing upward of 1,100 pounds have been taken by hunters over the years.

Alaska has its share of black bears, too, but black bears are usually fairly shy, somewhat retiring creatures that frequently go out of their way to avoid humans, generally preferring to remain in cover. Never take a black bear for granted, however. During my hunting days, I learned that black bears are tenacious and can be vindictive. Actually, more humans are injured by black bears than by browns, but that's another story.

All bears are unpredictable. A bear that sees a group of anglers might walk toward them just to show it owns this piece of the river, or then again, it might duck back into the alders never to be seen again. Some brownies will pretend they don't see you, and some actually don't until they smell you, and only then are they able to determine that you're human and not just another bear. What they do after they make their determination is anybody's guess.

The main thing to remember if you come in contact with an Alaskan brown bear is to keep your cool. Chances are more than likely that the bear has encountered other fishermen in previous seasons. It is always important to treat each bear with respect and keep out of its way. Walk slowly and give bears plenty of room, but *never run,* as predators often react by chasing. Always move away calmly and slowly. Most bears go to lengths to avoid human contact. Other bears, however, seem to go out of their way to demonstrate their superiority in an area. Such a bear will walk slowly in an angler's direction, acting as if it hasn't noticed any other living creature. But the game is over when the angler moves slowly away, talking to the animal in a low tone as he does so, giving the right-of-way to the owner of the real estate.

If you're thinking about bringing a firearm along, know that bears are very easy to wound but extremely difficult to kill. Consequently, it's generally better to leave the firearm at home and afford bears the right-of-way.

Several years ago, four of us were flown from King Salmon to a lovely little dry-fly flow, just where a wild, pretty creek enters a large lake, to do a little dry-fly fishing for rainbows and arctic grayling. As we circled the area in preparation for landing, our pilot spotted a brown bear sow and her two cubs standing at the mouth of the stream we wanted to fish.

"Oh, don't worry, she'll go away," the pilot said as he cut the throttle and lowered the flaps. "Just shout at her when you get to the mouth of the creek and tell her to go find another fishin' spot! She'll skedaddle."

A few minutes later, after we'd off-loaded our gear, the pilot told us he'd return in about four hours and flew off over the horizon.

The four of us stood there on that lonely beach, with only the sound of the nearby stream breaking the silence of that wilderness setting. Glancing over our shoulders, we could still see that brown bear sow and her two cubs fishing for sockeyes at the head of the riffles just 50 yards away.

Now all we needed to do was to rig our rods, assemble our gear, and then mosey over and kick the sow and her cubs out of *our* fishing hole. Sounds simple, right?

The four of us took turns yelling at the bears at the top of our lungs. Not one of the bears moved in the slightest or indicated that they had even noticed us. Could the bears hear us over the sound of the rushing stream? We didn't know. So, we started fishing. Not exactly where we *wanted* to fish, mind you, but over more toward the lake, hoping maybe we could find some arctic grayling over there. We didn't.

About an hour and a half later, to complicate matters further, another bear, a curious, three-year-old male, showed up and began snooping around the little bay, effectively herding us fly fishers—standing nearly chest-deep in water by this time—around like a bunch of dumb, wet cattle. Once, the curious bear even poked his head through some bushes not 20 feet from us, glared right at us, laid his ears back some, and then slowly retreated back into the scrub.

The clincher came about a half hour later. We could hardly believe our eyes as we stood there in water up to our armpits, able to observe every move the bears made.

Casually, inquisitively, one of the cubs wandered along the beach to the spot where, three hours earlier, we had piled our extra gear. The cub started sniffing around our rod tubes and packs, and after a minute or two, having finally realized it was whiffing human scent, the cub stood up, squealed just like a brown bear cub is supposed to squeal, and began hissing.

Instantly, Mama and the other cub ran over to protect the "endangered" cub, and all three bears snorted and danced around, frantically looking in all directions. A few seconds later, as if on cue, all three bears wheeled around and hightailed it back into the thick overgrowth.

Apparently, over the course of nearly four hours, the sow and her cubs hadn't even realized we were there until Junior had finally wandered over and smelled us—even though the four of us had been standing only a short distance from them yelling as loud as we could. It's entirely possible that those bears had never even seen a human before. Come to think of it, it *was* a fairly remote location we'd been dropped off at that morning.

Today, looking back on that situation, I'm willing to bet that sow and her two cubs simply took the four of us as being other bears until they got a whiff of human scent. Maybe all those stories one hears about bears being half blind are true, but one thing is for certain: Bears' noses don't lie.

On another occasion, on my first visit to Lower Talarik Creek with a lodge owner from the Iliamna area, I was in the middle of my first backcast when a brown bear sow stood up on her rear legs just 40 yards from me and began snapping her teeth. Instantly, I felt the blood drain from my head, and my pulse quickened considerably.

The sow just stood there on her rear legs, looking directly at me, snapping her teeth and frothing at the mouth. Suddenly it dawned on me that I had inadvertently wandered into her little breakfast nook—

completely unannounced—and this sow wasn't in the mood for fun and games that morning.

With no place to go, and realizing I didn't dare make any quick moves, I simply stood my ground and tried to smooth over whatever it was that I had done to upset Mama: "Hey, bear . . . hey, bear. . . . Everything's okay! . . . I'm just a lowly fisherman. . . . Don't mean you any harm. . . . Just out here lookin' for a few rainbows is all. . . . Don't even want any of your salmon!"

I glanced down at my 3.75-ounce fly rod, wishing it was a .375 H&H Magnum, when the sow suddenly dropped to all fours and out of my line of sight. This was the *really* scary time for me. I knew she was either coming for me or had retreated back into the scrub. What had I done to upset her so? I wondered. And where the hell was she?

Amazingly, about a minute later, *four* bears splashed their way across the creek not 40 yards upstream from me, and it was only then that I realized Mama had had three cubs with her all the while, none of which I could see from where I stood. Somehow I had inadvertently walked right up on all four of those bears, and Mama had become, should we say, a little protective.

Bears can do crazy things at times that don't seem to make any sense. Once, while four of us were fishing an unnamed stream in the Kukaklek Lake area, we spotted a blond bear standing on its hind legs, gazing at us from about 80 yards away. All four of us yelled at the bear, demanding it to take a walk, and it eventually dropped to all fours and began ambling away, just like a good bear should.

About fifteen minutes later, however, one of our party noticed a blond bear seemingly headed for the next county, apparently running as fast as it could run, in the *other* direction. Was it the same bear? If so, what had caused it to run?

What had happened, we eventually surmised, was that the bear, which had initially stood and gazed at us for seemingly a full five minutes, had, in its wanderings, crossed the prevailing wind currents, which revealed our human scent. The bear panicked, reacting by running as fast as it could, apparently right out of the territory. I'm willing to bet we were the first humans the bear had seen that year.

On another occasion, I was at Brooks Lodge at Katmai with guide Nanci Morris and a couple of her clients. Nanci suggested that a group of us take a little jaunt over to where the path follows the river and look for fish before returning for lunch. We all thought it was a splendid idea, and we'd made it about halfway down the main trail when suddenly a mature brown bear appeared from the bushes not 10 feet in front of us and entered the very path we were on.

Upon seeing the bear, Nanci stopped and signaled for the rest of us to do likewise, silently raising a finger to her lips, and stood there smiling at the sight of the huge creature. Seeming totally unaware of our presence, the huge beast continued to saunter down the path. Then yet another brown bear materialized from out of the bushes off to our right. It was about all any of us could do just to stand there, gawking in disbelief at the sight of those two 800-pound brown bears strolling along the path directly in front of us.

A minute or two later, fortunately, both bears wandered off the path a few yards. Seeing the possibility of passing them, our little group began making our way along the path once again in an effort to reach the pontoon bridge. After all, we were on a fish-finding mission, so despite two fully mature brown bears, Nanci Morris was bound and determined to find fish.

After we finally made it to the bridge, I turned and looked back, and to my astonishment, those two huge bruins were still over in the bushes just a few yards away, copulating. By this time, Nanci was far too busy pointing out any and all spots holding salmon to be concerned with the bears. Always the professional, she was doing what any experienced Alaska fishing guide would be doing under those circumstances—distracting her clients.

Bears depend on their sense of smell much more than their vision to authenticate human encounters, and they simply want to be given enough space to roam about. Consequently, the vast majority of encounters with bears in Alaska are entirely harmless. At times it seems as if both species simply have to put up with the other, but fortunately, both generally seem to want to maintain as much distance as possible, all the while attempting to maintain some degree of dignity in the process.

Some Alaska fly fishers seem to have the ability to disregard bears altogether, although most of us generally become a little concerned whenever a bear the size of a grand piano enters the picture. I'm pretty much in the middle, I'd guess. Some days I feel cool and collected out on the stream, fairly unconcerned about the presence of bears, but other days I might have to talk to myself a little, trying to focus on the fishing and dismissing any thoughts of bears.

A lot of any typical bear encounter is psychological, most agree; this is why the majority of Alaska's professional fishing guides never seem to be overly concerned about the presence of bears. Of course, you occasionally encounter one of those macho-type visitors who like to pretend bears never phase them in the slightest, especially when they get back to the lodge in the evening. The way I see it, however, anyone who isn't in the least concerned with the close presence of an 800-pound omnivore—one that is entirely capable of pulling down a bull moose—is either a fool or a liar, or he has an overblown ego in addition to being a combination of the other two.

Brown bears occasionally make it into Alaska's populated areas. At communities like King Salmon and Tok, for example, seeing an 800-pound brown bear wandering across the outskirts of town is fairly commonplace. And although people like to view Anchorage as being a fairly large, modern city—a place where you can drive down paved streets, mostly, and sometimes even experience cultural delights such as operas and concerts—federal game authorities are called on every now and then to drive over to one of the local elementary schools, pull a .375 H&H Magnum out of the trunk, and level a stray *Ursus arctos* right there in the parking lot, right in front of a classroom of wide-eyed fifth graders. This happened just a few years ago, only a couple of blocks from our home.

This is not to say this sort of thing happens frequently, however, or that people should begin to view Alaska's bears as being man-eaters. Quite the contrary, in fact. Simply put, nine times out of ten, given adequate room to roam and wander about, Alaska's brownies usually keep to the business of doing what they do best: wandering about in search of salmon.

There is one very important thing to keep in mind when fishing around bears, however: *Do not* allow a bear to discover that you have a fish on your line. If this happens, break the fish off the line by snapping the leader. Do this by pointing your rod directly at the fish and tightening the line, quickly pulling straight back against a taut leader tippet. The last thing you want to have happen is to have an 800-pound brown bear suddenly gallop over to check out a newfound fishing hole, with you standing smack-dab in the middle of it. Also, don't kill fish or leave them hanging around your tent or campground, and don't carry fish in backpacks, unless you *want* to attract a furry visitor.

Always remember the following while in bear country: First, it's the bears' territory; fishermen are but visitors. And second, Alaska bears are primarily interested in one thing: fish. Bears have fish on their minds, not humans. Fish are what bears primarily depend on for food, and fish are what bears are constantly in search of, except in August, when they go off for a time to pick berries. They return to the rivers again in September for one last look around before seeking a den for hibernation come late October.

Be especially mindful of sows with cubs, always doing your best to maintain a distance of at least 100 yards. Be ever cautious not to step between a mother and her cubs, even if the cubs might be large enough to be adults but are, in fact, 400-pound two-year-olds. A sow is likely to interpret intervention by an angler as a direct threat to her cubs and she may charge.

Always treat bears with respect, and always allow them to maintain a certain degree of dignity. Alaska's brown bears are very proud animals. Do not mock bears, and don't get into staring contests with them; bears can interpret this as a threat. Always try to allow them wide passage. There will be times when you have to inform bears of your presence, either by hollering or by speaking softly. Usually, the distance of each encounter will dictate which tone of voice to use. Don't walk up on bears quietly and surprise them; talk loudly and make plenty of noise as you travel, especially when passing through thick, wooded country. Sing out loud to yourself, even if you might not sound exactly like Julio Iglesias. Some people who spend a fair amount of time in Alaska's wilderness settings wear tin cans on their belts with loose pebbles rattling around inside to alert bears. Others prefer to speak loudly as they travel through dense brush.

You won't encounter bears on every Alaska fishing trip. Some days and some areas of the state simply produce more bears than others. Guides will know how to handle most situations. Most bear encounters are entirely innocent, so always keep cool and always use good common sense.

Deciding whether or not to carry a rifle into bear country requires some discretion. Experienced rifle handlers may feel comfortable carrying a powerful, large-caliber weapon. Inexperienced marksmen, however, should realize that a wounded bear is a vindictive and highly dangerous creature. The average angler will reduce the chances of a mauling by leaving all firearms at home. In most cases, giving bears—especially sows and cubs—enough room to roam and to go about their fishing is the angler's best line of defense. If a bear encounter of the too-close kind does arise, pepper spray can be an effective deterrent. U.S. Forest Service field crews, for example, carry 16-ounce containers of 10% Oleoresin Capsicum, which is recommended as their primary defensive response to bears.

Remember: Never run, scream, or panic around bears. Chances are, any bears you encounter in Alaska have had numerous other encounters with humans in past seasons and will interpret you as being just another one of those strange creatures that don't necessarily represent competition for their fish. One thing is for certain: Alaska bear encounters always make for stimulating wilderness experiences.

PART THREE

Where to Go

CHAPTER EIGHT

Anchorage Outbound

 ONCE YOU'VE ARRIVED IN ANCHORAGE AND HAVE YOUR gear and equipment assembled, the next step is to get to where the ultimate Alaska fishing action is found. If it's the best of Alaska's fly fishing you're seeking—trophy rainbows and few other anglers—this will mean flying another 200 to 475 miles west-southwest to Alaska's famed Bristol Bay sportfishing region. It's definitely worth the extra time and effort to get there.

Flying out from Anchorage via commercial airliner, your journey will take you high over the pristine, snowcapped Iliamna Mountain Range, one of the most majestic mountain panoramas a traveler can experience. Several of these imposing peaks (many still active volcanoes) ascend from sea level to well over 10,000 feet.

If you are traveling to one of the Bristol Bay hubs, such as Iliamna, King Salmon, Dillingham, or Bethel, you will probably fly at something approaching 20,000 feet, far over the tops of both the Iliamna and Alaska Mountain Ranges, and cloud cover often will shield many of the panoramic views that can be had when flying via small aircraft. On the other hand, if few clouds are present, you can enjoy some of the most grandiose scenery from the advantage of increased altitude. Currently, Yute Air Alaska, ERA Aviation, Reeve Aleutian Airways, PenAir, and Alaska Airlines all provide excellent bush access.

If you're traveling via small aircraft at a lower elevation, chances are you'll fly through the rugged, glacially cut canyon called Lake Clark Pass. Assuming the weather is good, this fifty-minute flight through steep, rugged peaks offers one of Alaska's most impressive mountain panoramas. Lake Clark Pass is a natural canyon valley cut through the glacially carved mountains that separate the salt waters of Cook Inlet from the Lake Clark–Iliamna region. This flight basically follows the Tlikakila River drainage through 65 miles of rugged Alaska wilderness terrain, taking you over numerous wilderness glaciers, many of which are receding.

The aqua blue waters of Lake Clark mark the beginning of some of Alaska's premier fishing. The bush community of Port Alsworth, complete with runways and avgas, lies along the southern shore of Lake Clark, just across from the partially hidden, scenic Kijik region. The prodigious Newhalen River, a large outlet draining Lake Clark into Iliamna Lake, is one of the most fertile sport fisheries in southwestern Alaska, with large quantities of rainbows, char, and grayling, and scores of incoming sockeye (red) salmon during July.

Nearing the end of Lake Clark, approaching Six-Mile Bay, the float plane traveler can see the shimmering green, knee-deep waters of the beautiful Tazimina River flowing below to the port side. Diagonally across Six-Mile Bay from the Tazimina lies the native village of Nondalton, complete with a dirt airstrip that is capable of handling even very heavy commercial transport aircraft.

Whichever means of travel you take from Anchorage, it is astounding how quickly you leave "civilization" behind and begin to experience the remoteness of the *real* Alaska. On a clear day, if you strain your eyes, you may be able to make out Kodiak Island looming far off in the southern distance or some abandoned farmhouses at Point Mackenzie, across from Anchorage, but for the most part, all you will see is an expanse of rugged, very imposing snowcapped mountains lying dead ahead, a region pilots commonly refer to as "no-man's-land." Among these mountains are many prominent, still-active volcanoes, including Mount Spurr, the volcano that fairly blanketed Anchorage and south-central Alaska with a formidable layer of ash in the fall of 1992; Mount Redoubt, which last erupted in 1990, situated across Cook Inlet from Kenai; the impressive 4,000-foot Mount Augustine, which last erupted in 1986, located just off Bruin Bay; and the always majestic, constantly venting, 10,016-foot Mount Iliamna.

It's impressive scenery, all right, and there is hardly a scene in North America that can top the views this region of the state offers. When storm clouds accumulate, however, which is frequently the case, these flights can become particularly ugly, and even frightening on occasion, with visibility suddenly all but nil, forcing pilots to fly by instruments only. Unfortunately, in Alaska, such weather conditions can occur rather routinely.

Welcome to the great adventure of traveling to one of Alaska's premier wilderness regions to experience some of North America's ultimate fly fishing, come wind, rain, clouds, or those occasional and incomparable clear, sunny days—days that the fly fisher long remembers.

CHAPTER NINE

Iliamna Country

 BY THE TIME YOU CROSS AQUA BLUE LAKE CLARK, approaching the native village of Nondalton, if the weather is clear, you can gaze over to the port side and begin to make out the glimmerings of vast Iliamna Lake off in the southern distance. Directly in front of you flows the Newhalen River (rainbows, char, grayling, lake trout, red salmon), the major artery feeding immense Iliamna Lake. Welcome to famed Iliamna country, easily one of Alaska's most revered fly-fishing regions. The Iliamna region offers fly fishers everything from small, ankle-deep creeks to big, wide, robust, swift-flowing rivers, all of which can be teeming with salmon and trophy trout at times.

Iliamna is the second-largest freshwater lake in North America, with well over 1,000 square miles of surface area. The lake varies between 25 and some 30 miles in width and is about 95 miles in overall length. More than twenty world-class freshwater tributaries flow into it. The lake is surrounded by extremely rugged, rolling tundra and, to the northeast, large, frequently white-capped mountains.

Like other huge lakes, Iliamna creates its own weather systems. The weather can be sunny and clear in surrounding regions but stormy at Iliamna, or vice versa. It can become very windy around Iliamna, making flying small airplanes across this region a job for experienced pilots.

First-time adventurers to the region are frequently surprised to see seals living among the myriad islands dotting the shores surrounding Iliamna, a reminder that Iliamna Lake is directly connected to the salt waters of Bristol Bay via the prodigious Kvichak River (pronounced Kwee-jack), the massive outlet of Iliamna.

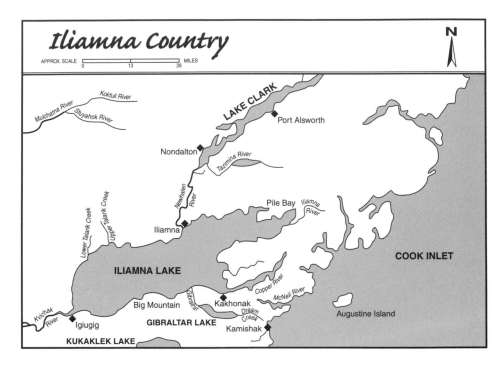

Iliamna country today is still every bit as good as its reputation, thanks in large part to catch and release, but also to the fact that some twenty world-class, not so easily accessed wilderness rivers and streams exist in these parts, giving visiting fly fishers a diversity of choice that protects any one area from overencroachment. Iliamna still qualifies as being a remote fly fisher's paradise, not so much because of its distance from populated regions as because of its sheer ruggedness. It's a place where several wilderness streams play host to better than decent numbers of trout and char, as well as Alaska's annual sockeye salmon run, an area of the state that—depending on the time of season—offers fly fishers up to ten different sportfish species to pursue on the fly.

Surrounding Iliamna Lake, there are many different fly-fishing adventures to be experienced: fly-outs over to the eastern coast for a go at halibut; fly-fishing for newly arriving salmon; or excursions to one of the area's clear-flowing wilderness rainbow and grayling streams or to the aquamarine, char-filled Iliamna River, with its lush, green surroundings.

The Iliamna River (char, some rainbows, grayling, lake trout, pinks, abundant red salmon) used to be one of Alaska's ultimate rainbow destinations. And fortunately, a smattering of rainbows still can be found in this lovely fishery today, despite the fact that only a few short years ago net fishermen overfished the river's rainbows. Despite its abundance of scrappy char, perhaps there is no better reminder in Alaska of the continued importance of employing strict catch-and-release tactics than the beautiful Iliamna River, for, contrary to what many first-time Alaska anglers tend to believe, Alaska's prodigious stocks of rainbow trout *are* subject to depletion. This is why it is imperative that *all* anglers (fly fishers as well as spin fishers) learn to appreciate and respect Alaska as being a last frontier of fishing and always practice catch and release whenever possible.

If you reach Iliamna country on August 5 or thereabouts, you will likely be able to pursue rainbow trout, arctic char, Dolly Varden, arctic grayling, northern pike, lake trout, and sockeye salmon. In even years more so than odd, the area also offers opportunities to cast to scores of feisty pink (or humpback) salmon. And if you're a bit lucky or if you stay on for a couple of weeks, you might even experience the beginnings of Alaska's prized silver salmon run.

It doesn't take fly fishers too long to begin dreaming of experiencing each of Iliamna's twenty-some alluring tributaries, like the picturesque, very wadable, seemingly made-for-fly-fishing Copper River (rainbow trout, Dolly Varden char, sockeye salmon, arctic grayling); the mile-long, very remote outlet called Gibraltar Creek (rainbow trout, sockeye salmon, Dolly Varden char); or that truly divine flow that forms Gibraltar Lake, appropriately named Dream Creek (rainbow trout, Dolly Varden char, sockeye salmon, arctic grayling). For many individuals experiencing this region for the first time, the list of Iliamna's truly world-class streams and rivers can seem nearly endless in number and utterly alluring. Some of Iliamna's waters are very large, deep rivers, but many are entirely wadable during most years, depending on the previous winter's snowfall and the amount of spring rains.

So where should a fly fisher interested in hooking into a few of Alaska's trophy rainbows and char (maybe even a rainbow in the 12- to 14-pound class) begin? I'd recommend beginning with either of the two major arteries in Iliamna country: the immense Kvichak River, the massive outlet of Iliamna Lake, the river that plays host to some of the world's most massive rainbows and largest runs of sockeye salmon; or the extremely fertile waters of the Newhalen River, that fast-flowing, extremely wide, partially wadable major Iliamna inlet that drains Lake Clark.

Before examining these two flows, let's first take a look at Alaska's annual rainbow trout cycle and the best way to fish these trout. During spring and early summer, before the salmon begin running, Alaska's rainbows concentrate on the only food sources available: sculpins, scuds, and leeches, and when the water temperatures begin to rise slightly, salmon and trout fry. Come July, however, scores of sockeye salmon suddenly appear in fresh water, and three to eight weeks later, drifting salmon eggs begin to appear by the hundreds of thousands. Alaska's rainbows and char soon begin following the migrating salmon, feeding on these loose, drifting salmon eggs awash in the currents. This is the time for fly fishers to switch to single-egg patterns and effectively begin matching this "hatch." Fishing these egg patterns employing floating lines with long leaders, with a split shot or two attached a foot or so up from the fly, and allowing the egg imitations to drift (if fishing from a drifting boat) along with the currents, will frequently lead to a high percentage of hookups.

By late August, when most of the salmon have spawned and begun to die, their loose, drifting, decaying flesh becomes a major food source for Alaska's predatory rainbows, grayling, and char. At that point, flesh patterns are especially effective. Alaska fly fishers sometimes combine single-eggs and flesh patterns. This is known as fishing steak and eggs.

The largest body of flowing water in Iliamna country is the mighty Kvichak, the major outlet of Iliamna Lake. At its origin, the flow is over 200 yards wide and 30 feet deep; 10 or 12 miles downstream, the river widens into partially wadable braids as it meanders into Bristol Bay. The outlet is usually exceedingly clear, allowing a fly fisher drifting in a boat to peer deep into waters that not only boast Alaska's largest runs of red salmon but also host many of the Great Land's exceptionally large— 17- to 19-pound—trophy rainbow trout.

Another of the most productive rivers in all of Iliamna country is the Newhalen, which definitely qualifies as "big water." For the best fishing success, you'll need to use appropriate big-river techniques. There are three preferred methods for the ultimate rainbow trout fishing on the Newhalen:

1. Fish the main channel from a drifting boat with a professional guide, letting your guide navigate while you cast and fish, concentrating on fishing.

2. Fish around invisible as well as visible islands, using a floating line and long leader and some split shot or lead wraps to get down deep, allowing your fly to imitate a swirling, drifting, sunken natural.

3. Wade out as deep as possible to seams and confluences, casting a

high-density shooting-head sinking or sinking-tip line (such as a Teeny T-300 or T-400), allowing a fly to swing through the currents just where waters of differing speeds converge and where lanes exist through which schools of migrating salmon pass. These are often the very spots where trophy trout and char will be found lurking, following their predatory instincts.

Another renowned tributary in the Iliamna region is Lower Talarik Creek. For years, anglers around the world have read in magazine articles and books about this hallowed, highly frequented Alaska fishery. And, yes, Lower Talarik continues to live up to its reputation. In fact, Lower Talarik is frequently good enough, regularly enough, that lodges in the Iliamna area often race each other to the stream in attempts to reach the choicest pieces of water first, sometimes a few guides and their clients even going so far as to erect tents in certain places at certain times, taking up temporary residency for a day or two and claiming temporary "rights."

Upper Talarik Creek—a completely separate stream, *not* the upper portion of Lower Talarik Creek—can also prove to be productive at certain times of the year, even though it hasn't achieved the reputation its sister has.

The Copper River, on the southern slopes along Iliamna Lake, winds its way down from Moose, Meadow, and Upper Copper Lakes, continues on down through Fog Lake, and eventually empties into Iliamna's beautiful, island-dotted Kakhonak Bay. This picturesque river is one of the loveliest flows I have ever fished, with long, velvety runs and swirling, glassy ribbons of pocket water. Flying over the river in a small bush plane, I could see groups of large rainbows finning just slightly downstream of pods of sockeye salmon. Fortunately, over the past few seasons, I've been able to fish the Copper on several occasions, and I've come to form a long-lasting, highly personal relationship with this flow, and with one hole in particular, where I've managed to take six or seven rainbows in the 6- to 8-pound range.

But this is only one of twenty or so near-celestial flows located in Iliamna country, most of which are wild, remote rivers that routinely produce rainbows in the 5- to 8-pound class.

Other streams that fairly beg for exploration include Pete Andrews and Tommy's Creeks. And fly fishers should not overlook the remote Koktuli (rainbows, char, grayling, lake trout, pike, kings, chums, reds, pinks, silver salmon), which eventually meanders into the remarkable Mulchatna (rainbows, char, grayling, lake trout, pike, kings, chums, reds, pinks, silver salmon). Both are located within an hour's flying distance of Iliamna. Also within reach of the Iliamna area is the exceedingly beautiful, clear-flowing Tazimina River (rainbows, char, grayling, red salmon), situated to the northeast of Iliamna, a made-for-fly-fishing drainage that eventually empties into Lake Clark's Six-Mile Bay. Nor should one overlook the adventure that goes with fishing the swift, remote, fairly logjammed and little-frequented Chilikadrotna (char, rainbows, grayling, lake trout, pike, kings, chums, reds, pinks, silver salmon). At certain times of the year, depending on the salmon runs, each of these Iliamna-country rivers offers truly world-class fly fishing.

Most of the fishing lodges in Iliamna country are located on the northern shores of Iliamna, a good percentage of these based just at a small peninsula of land where "Slopbucket Lake" is used as a base of float plane operations. Ted and Mary Gerken's famed Iliaska Lodge exists here, as does the respected Talarik Creek Lodge, currently managed by veteran pilot-guide Bruce Johnson. There are also several excellent fly-fishing lodges in the southern Iliamna area, including Bob Cusack's Cusack's Alaska Lodge, Chris Goll's Rainbow River Lodge, and Greg Hamm's intimate Iliamna Bearfoot Adventures, located fairly near the native village of Kakhonak.

Fly fishers are best off employing the services of a professional lodge or guide services while spending time in Iliamna country. Given the variable weather conditions and the number of natural hazards that exist, a fly fisher simply wouldn't make it very far for very long without the assistance of a seasoned professional.

Yes, Iliamna is a popular region, all right. It's a region with some of the premier fly-fishing rivers on earth; a place that, when the weather is good, is one of the premier fly-fishing regions in the world.

CHAPTER TEN

Katmai Land

DESPITE ITS FAMED AND WIDESPREAD POPULARITY, ALASKA'S Brooks River (rainbows, char, grayling, lake trout, reds, silvers) probably wouldn't rank as many fly fishers' first choice. However, the Brooks definitely would have to rank right up there with the best of them. All of its flows considered, the Brooks River, located in Katmai National Park at the head of the Alaska Peninsula, approximately 260 miles southwest of Anchorage and twenty-two minutes by float plane from King Salmon, must be considered one of Alaska's top ten fly-fishing destinations.

Any fly fisher who has experienced the Brooks would likely classify this flow as being one of Alaska's most picturesque rivers, especially where those crystal-clear waters spill from the pristine Lake Brooks, 1½ miles upstream from turquoise Naknek Lake.

On a clear day, the Brooks River looks as if its heavenly flow had been created solely to represent the ultimate rainbow trout stream for a full-color feature film.

The very first rainbow I hooked at Brooks, just down from Lake Brooks, was a 14-inch fish that amazed my companion and me by leaping 8 feet out of the water after torpedoing to attack the Bitch Creek wet fly I'd been drifting through the currents. Yet whenever I think of the beautiful Brooks, somehow I can't help but be reminded of the afternoon that a one-eyed, densely spotted, 8-pound rainbow trout hen attacked my black Electric Woolly Bugger so vigorously that she nearly ripped my 6-weight fly rod from my hand. For a moment I thought a bear had claimed my fly!

Nobody knows the secrets of hooking trophy rainbows at Brooks better than Brooks Lodge manager Perry Mollan, so I decided to check

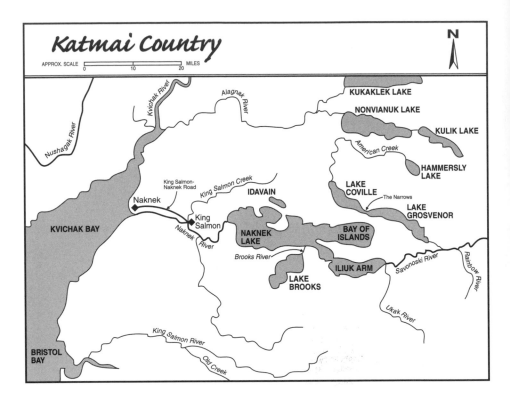

with him concerning the best river conditions for experiencing the Brooks. "*Any* day is a good day to fish at Brooks," he said. "In fact, just the other evening I landed an 8-pound rainbow that I hooked on a size 16 Parachute Adams, just around the corner, over by the cut bank."

Even with all the bears that are encountered at Brooks, especially in July, up near the falls, down by the oxbow lake, and by the pontoon bridge, the fishing experience is excellent. With its dense population of heavily spotted rainbows, numerous lively, graceful arctic grayling, and terrific sockeye salmon fishing during July and into August, Katmai's Brooks River offers fly fishers an unforgettable taste of some of Alaska's best fishing (which can depend more than a little, I've come to learn, on the water temperature at Brooks at any given time). Katmai is also supreme char country, as well as an excellent region for lake trout.

Besides the Brooks River, the Katmai region has several other world-class fisheries. Grosvenor Lodge, where the waters of lovely Lakes Coville and Grosvenor meet, remains an excellent choice, with its rustic solitude and a well-rounded variety of fishing opportunities, including 6- and 7-pound rainbows swirling around with the currents just steps away from the lodge.

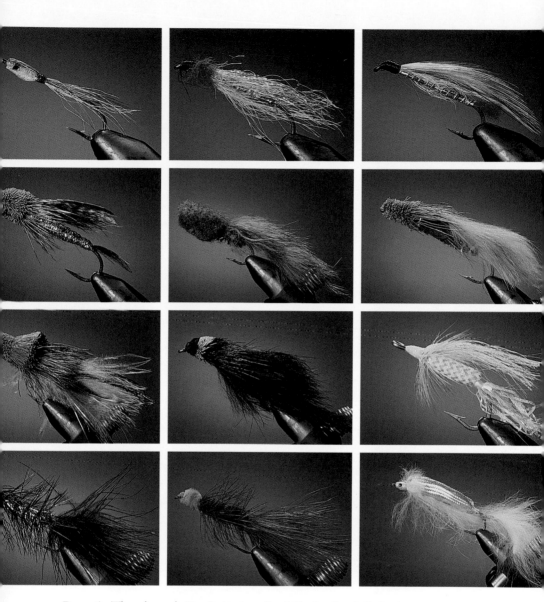

Row 1: *Thundercreek Fry Imitation, Fry/Alevin, Smolt Imitation*
Row 2: *Muddler Minnow, Wool Head Sculpin, Oversize Sculpin Pattern*
Row 3: *Dahlberg Diver, Sculpin/Leech Pattern, Everglo Fly*
Row 4: *Electric Woolly Bugger, Egg-Sucking Leech, White Zonker*

Row 1: *Egg/Flesh Fly, Karluk Flash Fly, Battle/Bunny Variation*
Row 2: *Flesh Fly, Sparkle Shrimp Variation, Krystal Bullet*
Row 3: *Teeny Nymph, Showgirl and Popsicle Streamers, Single-Egg Fly*
Row 4: *Champagne Egg Fly, Goddard Caddis, Griffith's Gnat*

Row 1: *Renegade Dry, Royal Wulff Dry, Black Ant Dry*
Row 2: *Elk-Hair Caddis, Irresistible Dry, Stimulator Dry*
Row 3: *Double Humpy Dry, Gold-Ribbed Hare's Ear Nymph, Deer Hair Mouse*
Row 4: *Antelope Hair Mouse, Polly Wog or Wog, Atlantic Salmon Fly (for comparison)*

A fall day at south central Alaska's Kenai River, where fly fishers will find rainbow, Dolly, king, sockeye, and silver salmon.

Piper Super Cubs, either on floats or wheels (as pictured here), carry only a pilot and one passenger, but are the ultimate aircraft for transporting fly fishers to Alaska's most remote fly-fishing waters.

Few fly fishers employ cane rods for fly-fishing Alaska, but the author still uses a bamboo rod at times for dry-fly fishing to grayling and rainbows, as shown here on the Agulowak River, just downstream from Wood River Lodge.

The author at Brooks River with "Henri-etta," the one-eyed, 8-pound rainbow hen that nearly ripped the fly rod from his hands when she went for his Electric Woolly Bugger.

Bill Herzog caught and released this spectacularly-spotted 9-pound rainbow trout while fishing a big, bulky black leech pattern at the "Braids" of the Alagnak.

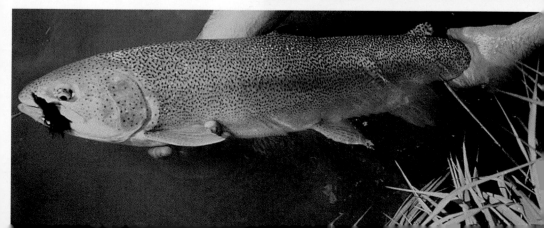

"Mousing" a floating deer hair or antelope hair mouse pattern to selected seams, riffles, and cutbanks often produces exciting results, as witnessed by this photo of one of several "leopard" 'bows the author hooked and released one afternoon while fishing out of Alaska West, part of the Aleknagik Mission Lodge operation on the Kanektok River.

While fly-fishing the Ugashik Narrows, the author caught this 12-pound "lemon char" while nymphing a champagne-colored Glo-Bug on a 6-weight graphite rod.

(right) With beautiful, subtle colorations and vermiculated markings, lake trout rank among Alaska's loveliest sport fish. Paul Rotkis displays a beautiful lake trout taken on a White Zonker near Nonvianuk Lake, while fishing out of Kulik Lodge.

By late August the majority of the millions of Pacific salmon that enter Alaska's fresh water annually to spawn have begun to die off, but their eggs and drifting, decaying flesh play an important role in maintaining the survival of Alaska's indigenous species..

Fly fishers and bears often fish the same waters for sockeye salmon, the bears' primary food. If you find yourself in this situation, remain calm, break off any fish you might have on the line, and back off quietly, giving the bears, especially sows with cubs, sufficient distance.

Fishing a dry fly at a small, pristine roadside lake on the Kenai Peninsula.

Regardless of the numbers of fish we catch, we who venture to Alaska's wild rivers experience scenic panoramas and vistas that form indelible, lifelong impressions.

Mike Mills displaying a trophy rainbow hooked and released on the Naknek River.

MICHAEL MILLS

Typical arctic grayling taken on a small, dark dry fly. With beautiful, flowing dorsal fins and subtle hues and colorful markings, grayling provide fly fishers with a delightful alternative.

The author with a 13-pound, 31½-inch trophy rainbow taken on a standard, size-4 Egg-Sucking Leech and a Teeny T-200 fly line, while fishing out of Mike Cusak's King Salmon Lodge.

Alaska's true "leopard rainbows," a unique subspecies of densely spotted Alaska rainbow trout, are much sought after by fly fishers known as "rainbow fanatics."

GREG SYVERSON

Southeast Alaska is famed not only for its scenic coves and bays, but also for the quaint and picturesque seaside towns and villages, represented here by "old town" Ketchikan.

In late summer, remote high-country wilderness tributaries often yield exceedingly large rainbow, such as the 28½-inch, 12-pound beauty the author admires here.

Trey Combs displays one of the several typical Alagnak 'bows he caught on the "Braids" of the Alagnak River, a broad, intertwined flow of excellent wilderness rainbow water.

Dollies and arctic char, which were unpopular a few decades ago for consuming too many salmon eggs, are now much in demand.

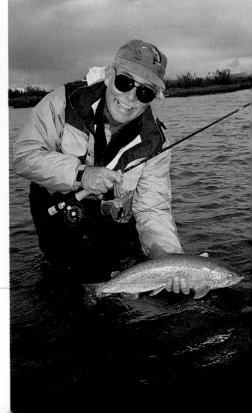

Several scenic mountain lakes north of Anchorage, in the Talkeetna Mountains, and others in the Kenai Range in south central Alaska offer Alaska fly fishers great day-trip opportunities.

GREG SYVERSON

ROBERT OLSON

This closeup illustrates the changes in color and shape that occur soon after spawning sockeye salmon enter Alaska's freshwater. The hooked kype, parrot-green head, and vivid red body color indicate the fish has been in fresh water more than a week.

Nanci Morris, a guide with Katmai Fishing Adventures, displays a large Naknek River rainbow.

The author at a difficult-to-access tributary south of Iliamna, with a memorable, mid-September, 9-pound rainbow that provided not only an honorable battle but also very nearly spooled his reel before being released.

The area adjacent to Kulik Lodge, located between Kulik and Nonvianuk Lakes within the boundaries of Katmai National Park and Preserve, features some of the premier rainbow, char, lake trout, and sockeye salmon fishing in the state.

Jim Teeny, well-known for his successful exploits with Pacific salmon and steelhead, shown here with a trophy chinook—or king salmon—that he brought to hand while fishing one of his series of excellent integral shooting-head fly lines.

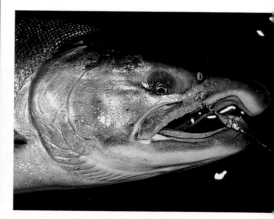

Jerry Donaldson displays a large, 18-pound chum salmon, also known as "Dog Salmon," that he managed and released while fishing on the Alagnak with his 9-weight.

Silver, or coho, salmon, such as the one shown here, are powerful and acrobatic adversaries on a fly rod and are welcomed Alaskan visitors every August.

A deHavilland Beaver taking-off from the Alagnak River. Easily Alaska's premier fly-fishing bush plane with its powerful engine and roomy interior, a Beaver can carry a pilot, six adult passengers, and all their gear.

The author, on the Goodnews River in western Alaska, displays one of the fifty or so sea-run Dollies he managed and released one day by skating simple fry patterns and drys along shallow seams and riffles.

Northern pike, known as "predators of the tundra swamp," can be found in Alaska's many tundra lakes and backcountry sloughs.

South central Alaska steelheads are typically somewhat smaller than those found in many of southeast Alaska's rivers, but this 18-pound steelhead caught and released by Bob Whittenberg on the Anchor River is trophy class.

This beautiful 6 to 7-pound Copper River rainbow was caught with a single-egg (Glo-Bug) imitation, then quickly photographed with one of the small, efficient cameras which are essential to fly fishers who practice catch and release.

The author dry-fly-fishing for arctic grayling on a relatively clear Susitna drainage that empties into the big and often silty Yentna River.

For centuries many of Alaska's native peoples have relied heavily upon Pacific salmon as a source of survival. This cache of drying salmon is different from most others in that it is protected from bears and other predators by a modern chain-link fence.

Pink salmon, or "Humpies," such as the typical male pictured here, are relatively easy to catch on a fly and will frequently take brightly colored offerings.

Fly fishing for rainbows can be even better over Kulik way. In fact, there are two particular streams near Kulik Lodge that bring back memories of leaping rainbows gulping at fry imitations at the surface during spring runoff and of several days where the taking of forty or even fifty fish was commonplace.

Other world-class flows in the Katmai region include Battle Creek, a fairly deep, fairly difficult-to-access, relatively difficult-to-fish, and always iffy rainbow stream that flows into the Narrow Cove of Kukaklek; the mighty Naknek River (rainbows, char, grayling, lake trout, kings, reds, pinks, chums, silver salmon), which flows directly past the community of King Salmon; and the outlet of Nonvianuk Lake. Another wonderful river is the Alagnak, or Branch (rainbows, char, grayling, lake trout, kings, reds, chums, pinks, silver salmon), a big, widely braided drainage that is the culmination of the outlets of both Kukaklek and Nonvianuk Lakes, journeying some 65 miles across the tundra, eventually joining up with the Kvichak 4 to 5 miles upstream of where it spills into Bristol Bay.

There are several other, lesser-known, although worthy flows that also deserve attention, most of them remote, wilderness flows. These include the Grosvenor River (numbers of hearty char) before it becomes the Savonoski River (rainbows and char); the wild, seemingly always bear-infested Hardscrabble (char, lake trout, red salmon) and Contact Creeks (rainbows, char, reds, pink salmon); the seldom-fished, brushy, and also very beary Idavain and Margot Creeks, both near Brooks; and the tundra-etched Nanuktuk Creek, which flows into Kukaklek (a fly fisher should be prepared to hike a few miles to experience this stream's finest waters). Each of these remote Katmai fisheries ranks as a superb fly-fishing destination, and each warrants the supervision of a professional guide.

Alaska's Katmai region also includes Katmai National Park and Preserve, a vast 4-million-square-acre tract that begins some 20 miles south of Iliamna. In general, it is lusher, greener, and more densely forested than Iliamna. This area is dotted with lakes, some of which are frequented by man, but many of which have never seen human footprints.

Within the park, there are dozens of lesser-known streams that are enticing to explore with a guide and a fly rod, each making for a fine, exciting day of north-country fly fishing, whether it happens to feature premier fishing opportunities for rainbows or for char.

Many of the rainbows in Katmai seem to be a unique subspecies, sporting impressive pinkish maroon stripes, magenta-tinted gill plates, and dense, dark spots over much of their bodies (hence the nickname leopards), and they are some of the most striking rainbows to be found in Alaska.

At the northernmost region of Katmai National Park and Preserve flow the wild-country "braids" of the wondrous Alagnak—a multi-ribboned drainage stretching some 25 miles until it joins together again. At certain times of the year, especially during mid-June and September, the braids can be a rainbow trout fly fisher's dream come true (particularly when water levels from Nonvianuk and Kukaklek Lakes are moderate), making for some of the finest combination wet-and-dry-fly fishing to be found anywhere in the state. Mousing for rainbows (using floating mouse imitations tied with deer or antelope hair) at the braids often makes for superlative fly fishing. On warm June days before the salmon arrive, the fly fishing for rainbows and grayling at the braids can be extraordinary. And come late August, fishing at the braids again is excellent, with numbers of hungry, boldly spotted, magenta-hued rainbows, along with the possibility of bright, acrobatic coho (or silver) salmon.

The braids begin just where the forks of the outlets of Nonvianuk and Kukaklek Lakes join together, some 35 miles above Tony Sarp's Katmai Lodge, approximately midway on the Alagnak. Downstream, beginning in mid-July, there is large-scale salmon action as vast numbers of chum and king salmon migrate from the salt waters of Bristol Bay.

Anglers are frequently surprised to learn that the Alagnak qualifies as a superb king salmon fishery at times. The middle and lower portions of the Alagnak, particularly alongside steep cut banks, offer some of the best places for locating numbers of 25- to 50-pound Bristol Bay kings. And beginning in late July, when fishing the extremely wide lower flats of the Alagnak (4 or 5 miles up from its confluence with the Kvichak), fly anglers will also discover superb chum and pink salmon fishing. Frequently, fly fishers stripping pink and/or purple Popsicle Streamers or Show Girls through these wide shallows of the Alagnak experience some spectacular, powerful takes that serve to instantly educate as to the strength of a 20-pound chum salmon. On this lower portion of the Alagnak, 9- and 10-weight fly rods are highly advised.

For those fly fishers desiring superb trophy (28- to 31-inch) rainbow trout fly fishing, there are few better choices in all of southwest Alaska than the Nonvianuk-Kukaklek-Alagnak system, including many areas of the braids of the Alagnak. Here you can get out of a boat and wade, whether you fish just downstream of an island to a fairly deep seam or confluence, using a sculpin or a leech pattern, or go with a dry fly along stretches of long riffles, or fish a weighted Flesh Fly or perhaps a single-egg imitation, using a floating line and a long leader with a split shot or two crimped just above the fly, making for a very natural-appearing downstream drift. Upstream several miles, at Nonvianuk Lake's headwaters, are such notable waters as Kulik Lake and the Kulik River, the site of famed Kulik Lodge.

Over the seasons, many experienced, world-renowned fly fishers have come to appreciate (and frequently written about) other blueribbon Katmai waters, such as the widely revered American Creek (rainbows, char, grayling, lake trout, red salmon), a highly wadable, allbut-invisible, 26-mile flow that drains panoramic Hammersly Lake, which is located high in the snowcapped Walatka Mountains. Eventually the American winds its way down and around the hillside, emptying into the lovely, undefiled Lake Coville. Then, after passing through Coville and constricting through "the Narrows," just where Grosvenor Lodge is located, the flow forms the beginnings of the panoramic, 17-mile-long, mountain-surrounded Lake Grosvenor.

Like all fly fishers who have experienced Alaska's scenic Katmai region, over the seasons I've formed some indelible memories of the place, such as the exceptional fishing that can often be experienced at the picturesque outlet of exceedingly clear Hammersly Lake, where, until mid-July or thereabouts, fly fishers arrive to snow-packed beaches surrounding the lake, making for a sight of spectacular beauty. Just at the outlet of Hammersly, and for the next 5 or 6 miles downstream, as the American Creek carves its way downhill to Lake Coville, the creek offers some of the loveliest pocket water I've had the pleasure of fishing.

Thanks largely to the practice of catch and release, the American Creek still offers superb fly-fishing opportunities, and many fly fishers continue to be delighted with this region of Katmai. Good numbers of hungry char, rainbows, and grayling exist there, and the fish frequently will strike at any number of patterns—wet or dry—that a fly fisher might present.

Another excellent Katmai fishing experience is the Bay of Islands, located at the northeast corner of sizable Naknek Lake, just a few miles distant from Brooks. The Bay of Islands is a remote, spectacularly scenic, island-dotted region of a pristine, less frequented lake where rainbows and lake trout in the 10- to 15-pound range can be hooked and released. This spot ranks among Alaska's most highly regarded waters.

The Katmai region, with its sapphire blue lakes, spruce green forests, and majestic mountains, has some of the loveliest, wildest rivers in North America. Truth is, a person could spend a lifetime fishing and exploring the wondrous, 4 million-square-acre labyrinth of untamed drainages called Katmai.

CHAPTER ELEVEN

Wood River–Tikchik Lakes Region

NESTLED DUE WEST OF THE ROLLING MUKLUNG HILLS, which rise slowly and steadily from a huge, barren, scenic Alaska tundra, lies the famed Wood River–Tikchik Lakes region, which consists of eleven lakes and their interconnected rivers and easily ranks as one of the Great Land's best fly-fishing destinations. If ever there was a haven for the fly fisher, particularly for the dry-fly fisher, it's the Woods River–Tikchik Lakes region.

One of the beauties of the region is that it is not overfrequented by humans. Better yet, above-average numbers of rainbows, Dolly Varden and arctic char, and arctic grayling, as well as king, chum, sockeye, pink, and silver salmon in season, are commonly in Tikchik waters. Simply put, a fly fisher can experience the ultimate Alaska fishing adventure, in water fit to drink, with few, if any, competitors.

Dillingham serves as the primary jumping-off point for most fly fishers visiting the Tikchik region. Several premier Alaska fishing lodges are located in the area, and lodges typically meet newly arriving guests at either the jet-serviced Dillingham Airport or a few miles away at the lakeshore village of Aleknagik.

One of the beauties of a Tikchik fishing experience is the multitude of scenic, fjordlike coves, bays, and cul-de-sacs, many of these remote, seemingly never-before-explored areas offering the visitor a feeling of solitude. In fact, it's so easy for anglers to get away in these parts that it would be entirely possible for two groups of fishermen to fly to Dillingham together, be picked up by competing lodges, fish the same lakes and streams, and not see one another until they met up again for their return flight back to the Lower 48 a week later.

And experiencing excellent dry-fly fishing is nearly a given here. The region includes some of my favorite dry-fly waters in Alaska.

Well do I remember the first time I ever laid eyes on the lovely Agulowak, frequently referred to as "the Wok" for short. Here before me was a largely wadable, clearer-than-crystal river flowing at a perfect 3 to 5 knots, a flow with fish so abundant that the entire surface of the river was dimpled by rings created by numbers of rising rainbows and grayling. And down on the stream bottom, I could see multitudes of gray, ghostlike silhouettes, which turned out to be exceptional numbers of orange-and-pink-spotted arctic char. All in all, it looked like fly-fishing heaven!

My first cast, with an Adams Irresistible, was to no particular fish. At that point of the game, I was just trying to overcome my excitement long enough to form a decent loop. After I finally managed this, as I released the fly line and my fly gently fluttered to the surface and started to drift, almost immediately a 17-inch grayling glided up to the surface and inhaled my size 12 dry fly. Ten seconds after wading out into the lovely Wok, I realized we were in for some extraordinary fly fishing. The only frustrating thing was that I couldn't decide whether I should cast to rainbows or to grayling, or whether to add a split shot or two and go down for char.

Only recently I had the opportunity of dry-fly fishing for arctic grayling, fishing greased caddis patterns, on the Wind River, one of the northernmost flows in the Tikchik chain. It's a gem of a wild, clear-flowing stream that snakes its way through some spectacular mountain scenery, including dramatic background panoramas of cascading waterfalls. And although those grayling weren't as large as others I've encountered in Alaska, they were large *enough,* and best of all, they were plentiful. With their subtle, iridescent turquoise-and-pink-striped dorsal fins, those beautiful Tikchik-country arctic grayling would seemingly materialize out of nowhere and suck in a caddis or foam Black Ant pattern like it was their last meal. And as usual, most of the grayling takes occurred on the way back down.

On the Igushik, just south of the Tikchik Lakes system, a companion and I experienced superb char fishing. We took several stout, 4- to 5-pound char apiece, each of us swinging brown or olive Electric Woolly Buggers through big, burly water, using 200-grain sinking-tip lines. And this region of Alaska features many similar waters where excellent char fishing can be experienced.

Beginning at the north, Nuyakuk Lake (the location of Bud Hodson's

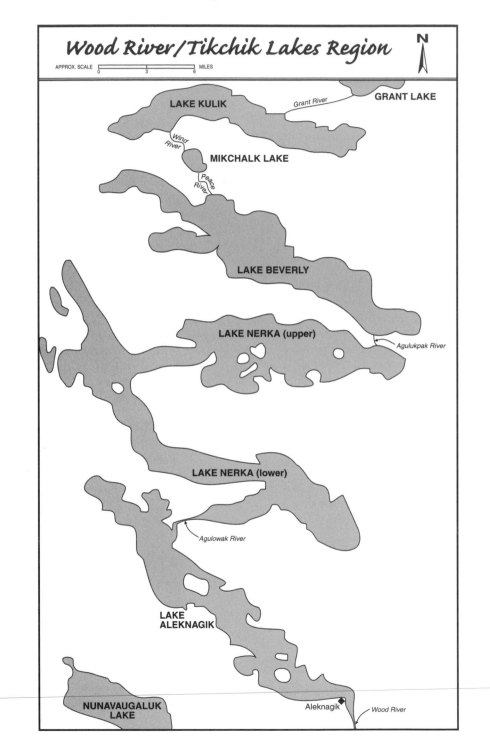

famed Tikchik Narrows Lodge) is the uppermost lake in the Wood River–Tikchik Lakes region. This lake is not connected via any major flow to the other lakes in the system, but drains eastward via the Nuyakuk River, eventually joining up with the big Nushagak, one of the major river drainages in the state.

The interconnected Tikchik Lakes system begins with the small but very clear and beautiful Lake Kulik, which drains via the lovely Wind River. A particularly delightful flow, this unique 3-mile stretch features nearby views of towering, majestic peaks and cascading waterfalls, as well as good numbers of fair-size rainbows and arctic grayling.

From there, the flow turns into Mikchalk Lake. Then the drainage becomes the 2-mile-long Peace River, before emptying into the large, 16-mile-long Lake Beverly. The famed, 2-mile-long Agulukpak River (called "the Pak" for short) connects Lake Beverly with large, wishbone-shaped Lake Nerka. Fly fishers would do well to spend some time fishing at the outlet of Beverly—the beginnings of the Pak—where numbers of rainbows, grayling, and char (not to mention sockeyes, in season) can be found.

At the still backwaters of Lake Beverly and Lake Nerka (both sizable bodies of water featuring many unfrequented cul-de-sacs), fly-fishing adventurers could easily spend a full day or two in search of northern pike, which can often be found in these lake-system dead ends. Fishing for pike can offer the exploring fly angler a wonderful change of pace for a few hours, fishing an 8-weight rod, making long casts, and stripping large, colorful flies such as Lefty's Deceivers or one of the excellent Dahlberg Diver surface offerings. With these, whether fishing at the surface or below, the fly fisher typically employs longish casts over near weed and/or lily beds. When retrieving these large, highly visible patterns by utilizing short, sharp strips, the fly fisher must always be ready for the sudden, voracious strike of a large *Esox lucius*.

The outlet of Lake Nerka forms the beginnings of the wonderful Agulowak River—the Wok. A few private cabins exist here, and visiting fly fishers should be careful not to invade the privacy of those who live here year-round.

After the Agulowak, the currents of the river lead into the tongue of lovely Lake Aleknagik, where teeming schools of hungry char (frequently indicated by flocks of screaming arctic terns and seagulls) often can be fished effectively via olive Woolly Buggers or common smolt offerings. The most effective method often is to fish a stripped-in smolt or streamer pattern very deeply on a high-density sinking-tip line. It can be great sport casting from a loose, drifting boat, swirling around with the shifting currents, knowing that more than likely, any moment now, a large, muscular char will come up and grab someone's fly.

There are several highly respected lodges in this region of Alaska, including Aleknagik Mission Lodge, near the southeast corner of Lake Aleknagik; Bristol Bay Lodge, on the far northwest shore of the Aleknagik; Wood River Lodge, at the outlet of Lake Nerka; and Crystal Creek Lodge, on the sizable Nunavaugaluk Lake, a large, beautiful body 7 miles to the southwest of Aleknagik that is not connected by any major tributary.

This region of Alaska holds many memories, such as the afternoon I almost lost my brand new, prized, state-of-the-art G. Loomis GLX 4-weight rod, not to mention one of matched pair of Hardy Marquis 5 reels.

We'd been anchored at a wide, fairly deep glide in the river, powering dry flies, making 50- and 60-foot casts to varying spots in the flow and taking medium-size, 3- and 4-pound rainbows on every third cast or so. I was throwing a size 8 Humpy, greased with floatant, and had been experiencing good success. It was exciting fishing, one person casting from the bow of the boat and one from the stern. From our elevated positions above the river, it was easy to watch our drifts and see the rainbows rise up through the crystalline currents as they'd leave their 4- and 5-foot-deep holding lies and head directly for our tantalizing, oversize dry flies.

We'd been hooking and releasing rainbows in this manner for an hour or so when I realized I was thirsty. So, with my dry fly left bobbing out in the currents some 60 feet downstream of the boat, I gently laid down my fly rod and reached for a soft drink. Just at that instant, a large rainbow suddenly clamped down on my distant dry fly, and my rod and reel flew out of the boat and disappeared.

"Quick! Let's pull anchor!" our guide hollered. "Maybe we can drift downstream and locate your rod."

Amazingly, a minute or so later, after we had pulled anchor and started the outboard, a few inches of my brilliant chartreuse Cortland fly line could be seen bobbing at the surface, along with the rod tip, and within another minute or two, our guide maneuvered the boat around to where I could reach out and barely grab the tip of my drifting fly rod. When I finally managed to turn the rod around, not only did I see that I had been lucky enough to have retrieved my expensive rod and reel, but by the tugging still evident at the end of the line, it also became clear that the fine, 4½-pound rainbow was still hooked!

Our guide quickly dropped anchor, and in another couple of minutes I was able to bring the fish up alongside the boat despite the steady, swift currents. I was just reaching for my camera, when that beautiful rainbow flipped the hook.

Yes, the Wood River–Tikchik Lakes system is a fly fisher's paradise, all right, and it's no secret that this pristine region qualifies as one of Alaska's ultimate fisheries. And by employing strict catch-and-release practices, we can help ensure that our children and grandchildren also will be able to enjoy world-class fishing there.

CHAPTER TWELVE

Western Alaska Rivers

 TWO OF ALASKA'S MOST RENOWNED RIVERS ARE LOCATED in the western part of the state: the Goodnews River, which empties into Goodnews Bay at Kuskokwim Bay, near the village of Goodnews Bay, and the Kanektok River (pronounced Connect-tok), which flows into the Bering Sea at the seacoast village of Quinhagak. Both rivers begin some 80 miles inland at backcountry lakes, in the rolling hill country of the Togiak Wildlife Refuge, before ending their meandering, downhill journeys to Alaska's far western coast.

The Goodnews and Kanektok are medium-small flows that are wadable in many places and provide many wonderful wade-and-cast opportunities. Both rivers offer the fly fisher a wide choice of good, varying water types, including deep, easy-flowing pockets, stretches of long, moderate-riffled runs, and shallow, glassy glides with sandy islands from which to cast. And both are regarded as premier Alaska fly-fishing rivers.

In season, both the Goodnews and the Kanektok offer the fly fisher opportunities for all five species of Pacific salmon—kings, sockeyes, chum, and pinks, along with spectacular silver fishing—plus good numbers of rainbows, arctic grayling, and fresh-from-the-ocean, sea-run char. The Kanektok is probably most noted for its superb king and leopard rainbow fishing, and the Goodnews for its char and trophy silvers.

Both of these rivers are worth any extra travel time or expense required to reach them. Like all rivers, however, each has its own distinct personality and only the individual fly fisher will be able to judge which of the two he considers superior.

Since I have yet to actually fish the Kanektok (although I've scheduled a trip and will have experienced its currents by the time this book gets printed), I am not able to report on that river firsthand. However, I've definitely heard good things about it from friends who've become addicted to fishing that river—and who return there summer after summer from points around the globe. My upcoming Kanektok adventure will be conducted through Alaska West, part of the Aleknagik Mission Lodge operation.

I *have* become fairly well acquainted with the lovely Goodnews, and without hesitation, I can recommend it as being one of the premier fly-fishing destinations in Alaska. The Goodnews River Lodge is a primary access to this silvery flow.

Over the years, I'd heard many good things about the Goodnews, but it took me seven long years of dreaming and scheming before I was able to finally wet my boots in western Alaska water.

I stayed at Ron Hyde's Goodnews River Lodge, a large, framed, deluxe tent camp, entirely fashioned on wooden supports. The tents are well heated and keep guests just as comfortable as if they were staying at a regular Alaska fishing lodge. Best of all, the lodge is only a stone's throw from the river.

The afternoon I arrived at camp, I had an hour or so before Ron Hyde and Bob Stearns, a contributing editor for *Field & Stream* magazine, as well as a couple of other clients, would be returning to camp. Consequently, there was little for me to do but wet a line, and on my very first cast out in front of the lodge, fishing my pet 9-foot, 4-weight graphite rod and a size 4 Egg-Sucking Leech, I felt a sudden, solid take and eventually succeeded—after a twenty-minute battle—in bringing to hand a beautiful, heavily spotted, 26-inch, 8-pound rainbow hen. "Not a bad way to start," I thought.

A half hour later, Ron, Bob, and a couple of other clients returned to camp, reporting that they had taken nearly sixty char on drys.

The next morning, Ron held a skating-fly clinic with a surface pattern he called a wounded fry. It was an alevin pattern that had been devised some years earlier by one of Ron's clients and has proven to be very effective over the seasons. It was a rather simple fry pattern that wasn't weighted but was tied lightly so that it could be skittered along the surface. Ron explained that the rainbows and char took it to be a wounded fry. It was fished by casting it dead across current, then feeding out slack, allowing the downstream currents to help form a big, intentional loop, and then pulling the fly dead across stream, using the rod tip

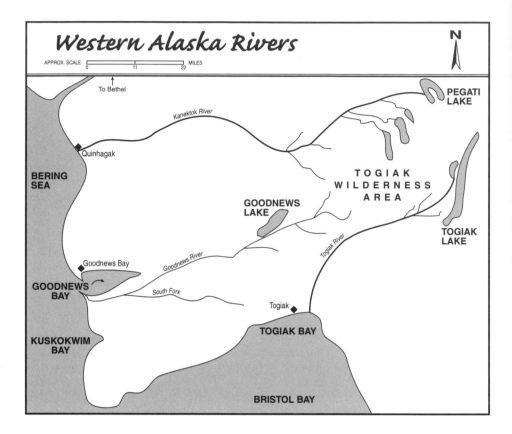

as an aid, with a very low, horizontal upstream pull. The fly would begin skating on the surface, and soon a fish or two would see the "wounded fry" and begin to follow it. The fish often create their own wakes as they come, and nine times out of ten the angler can see the strike coming before it occurs.

It didn't take me long to get the hang of Ron's across-the-current waking-fly technique, with results in the vicinity of fifty-plus char per day—on drys. It was barely August, and the silvery Goodnews seemed all but surreal at that time of year. Here and there we'd come across steep, 50-foot cut banks that frequently would shelter wide, shallow riffly spots just above a silky, glassy flow, moving at about a perfect 3 to 5 knots. These areas always seemed to hold hundreds of char.

Surprisingly, we never saw a single bear during my five days on the Goodnews, but then, it *was* between salmon runs at the time. We did see more than a few bear tracks on sandbars, but we never saw a steaming sign.

On my fifth and final day at the Goodnews (days number two through four having been occupied with dry flies and char), Ron, Bob, and I cruised downstream along the lower reaches of the river in search of silvers, probing about the lower, intertidal regions of the Goodnews.

Ron was all business—as usual while he's fishing—as he scoured the riffles with binoculars for any sign of fish. It was the second day of August, the time of year when fresh-from-the-ocean silver salmon begin to show themselves, but sadly, the final day of my dream-come-true trip.

"Just for fun, let's try the 'probe,' Bob," Ron said, "maybe over by that deep eddy just down from those willows a touch. I've got a feeling some silvers may have moved in during the night and might be holding in there."

He handed Bob the short spinning rod he kept near his steering console just for such occasions. Bob executed a good cast, landing the "probe" very near the spot Ron had indicated. Not expecting much, I quietly stood and observed as Bob methodically cranked the spinning-reel handle, expertly retrieving the deeply sunken jig.

Then, without warning, Bob's rod tip curled into a deep, heavy arch, the heavy-casting mono line firmly taut as if Bob had snagged up on a deep or unrelenting root, yet when Bob's reel suddenly began feeding out line, I realized that Bob had, indeed, hooked a fish on his very first cast.

I assumed that Bob had hooked a fresh silver. When I glanced over at Ron, he was smiling to himself, proud that his trusty old "probe" had completed yet another successful reconnaissance mission.

"This ain't no normal silver, boys," Bob muttered while steadily cranking. "If it *is* a silver, it's one trophy fish, that's for sure!" He continued pumping, straining, and reeling, playing that big fish for all he was worth.

Five minutes later, the fish was finally at the surface, and Ron reached out with a net. The fish seemed as large as a king salmon, and I wondered if the net could hold that much fish. Then I began to realize I was gazing at the largest rainbow trout I've ever seen in my life.

"Is *that* a rainbow?" I asked in astonishment.

"You'd better believe it," Ron said. He turned and grinned, straining with a fish that more than filled the salmon net. "I told you they grow 'em big down in these parts!"

"What do you think that fish weighed?" I asked Ron after he had released the fish.

"Hard to say, really," Ron mumbled. "It looked to be at least 37 inches in length, and I'd estimate it was somewhere around 21, maybe 22 pounds."

We did manage to take several silvers on the surface during the next couple of hours, skating pink Wogs in front of the incoming schools of salmon.

Unfortunately, four hours later we were back at the lodge, and soon I was packed and headed for one of the jet boats that would take me the 4 or 5 miles downstream to the village of Goodnews Bay and the airstrip. My five days at the Goodnews had passed quickly, and it was time to return to Anchorage.

CHAPTER THIRTEEN

The Alaska Peninsula

 THE ALASKA PENINSULA IS EASILY THE WILDEST, LEAST-frequented, least-disturbed fly-fishing region in the state today. The Peninsula is a vast, rugged, 700-mile-long finger of virginal wilderness, with turbulent mountain passes, miles of unexplored saltwater beaches, and countless unspoiled rivers and streams where char commonly grow to 10 pounds and silvers to 20, where sockeyes and chums run in the hundreds of thousands, and where competing anglers are rarely seen. It's a largely uncharted region where a fly fisher and his guide could wander about every day of every summer for the rest of their lives, forever sampling unfished waters, and never coveting another fishery in the state.

Active volcanoes still exist in the region, an integral part of what is sometimes referred to as the "Ring of Fire," a chain of volcanoes and geologic faults extending all the way from Alaska down through Mexico along the leading western edge of the always drifting North American continent. The famed Katmai National Park, with its Valley of Ten Thousand Smokes, is located at the northernmost part of the Peninsula.

Getting to the Alaska Peninsula is not always an easy task. There are few, if any, roads to be found in most parts of this sparsely populated wilderness region. There are no airports, but there are hundreds of gravel bars and miles of ocean beaches, as well as any number of remote lakes and tidal lagoons, upon which adventurous fly fishers and their pilots may attempt to land, weather permitting.

The weather to be found there generally isn't what you would describe as balmy, however. In fact, one former successful Alaska Peninsula bear and moose guide told me the reason he eventually abandoned

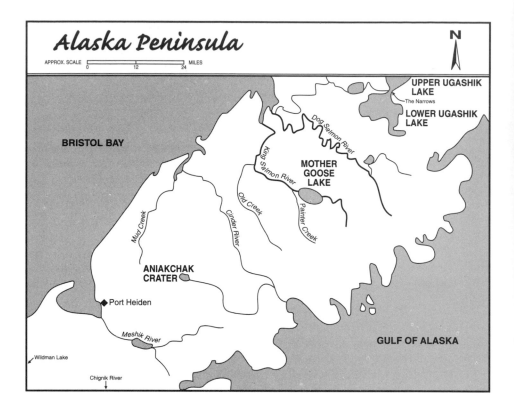

his trade was that he was tired of risking his life with all the flying required in this blustery, desolate, mountainous region. Simply put, the Peninsula definitely isn't a place for a weekend pilot.

Aside from the winds you can encounter on the Peninsula, one of the biggest obstacles is lack of gasoline. Avgas is sometimes available in small Alaska bush communities and native villages like Port Heiden or even Port Moller or Chignik, but not always; never on a guaranteed basis. And even if there is avgas to be found at one of these locations, it may already have been allocated. Truth is, you could spend hours flying across this vast, wind-parched region in a small airplane and not reach the halfway point to your destination (never seeing another human being in the process) before having to turn around again for lack of fuel.

The Becharof Lake region in the northern reaches of the Peninsula (an area known for its numbers of bears), fairly the southernmost of Alaska's regions hosting rainbow trout, can, at times, be a fly fisher's paradise. Much of the char, silver, and grayling fishing in this northern region of the Peninsula is superior, and there are also excellent opportunities, here and there, at dime-bright kings. The southern half of the Peninsula, however, has no rainbows, although talk of secret Alaska Peninsula steelhead streams is heard on occasion.

Some 25 miles south of Becharof lies the famed Ugashik Narrows, a 300-yard-long, heaven-made fishery running between Upper and Lower Ugashik Lakes. Today, it remains one of Alaska's most revered waters, and thanks largely to catch and release, arctic grayling and arctic char continue to be found in good numbers.

One lovely mid-September morning, two companions and I had those Ugashik currents all to ourselves for five celestial hours. Everywhere we looked, grayling the size of salmon were porpoising around us (just as Lee Wulff, years earlier, had described the place), and arctic terns and seagulls whirled and glided silently above the riffles. Those Ugashik currents were so clear that it seemed one of us could have flipped a quarter into those glassy riffles and been able to read the date from yards away. I remember thinking that they might as well post a sign there that reads: Caution: Holy Water! Spiritual Fishing Experience Awaits You—Proceed With Reverence.

After quickly hooking and releasing a couple of 19-plus-inch grayling, taken on a Griffith's Gnat, something told me to change flies to a single-egg pattern and wander out near where the outlet of the Narrows spills into Lower Ugashik Lake. Almost immediately after doing so, I felt the tug of what turned out to be a 32-inch, 13-pound arctic char. The fish proceeded to strip out nearly all of my backing as it headed for the deeper waters of the lake. Thirty minutes later, somehow I was able to manage that beautiful tangerine, pink, and orange over forest green char into the shadows and into my waiting grasp. Presently, my companions waded over to assist, one of them snapping a photo of me with that char, a photo that today represents much more to me than just another picture of a trophy fish.

I've also had the pleasure, on a couple of occasions, of float-planing in to others of these remote, unnamed northern Peninsula streams for a day's fishing. These adventures remain positive experiences in my memory, even though on one of them, we barely made it out when 50-mile-an-hour winds sprang up.

Most grayling I've encountered in these remote Peninsula regions have taken large, bulky caddis patterns or juicy-looking Griffth's Gnats. These fish averaged 18 inches, with several measuring up to 20 or 21 inches. Many had such huge girths that they were almost too large to grasp with one hand.

One doesn't always simply float-plane in to a nearby lake adjacent to these scattered Alaska Peninsula streams and begin fishing, however. Fact is, only a small percentage of Peninsula lakes are large enough to accommodate float planes much larger than Piper Super Cubs; consequently, many of the streams can be reached only by foot, slogging through soggy tundra swamps and negotiating extended areas of tussocks the size of fire hydrants. Never mind the brown bears one encounters on occasion in these tundra settings; truth is (especially if the trip occurs during June), it's the swarms of mosquitoes that can sometimes cause a fly fisher to wonder why he didn't take up billiards instead. But if the weather is decent, and if you do manage to access one of the better Peninsula streams, and if the wind isn't howling, and if your timing is right for the species you're pursuing, you will soon come to appreciate fly fishing once again.

Beginning in midsummer, many Peninsula creeks become chock full of bright kings, chums, silvers, and pinks, as well as those all-important Alaska "magnets," the sockeyes, the salmon species that, more than any other, serves to attract numbers of rainbows and char into shallow waters they otherwise probably wouldn't venture into. And later in summer, when the fishing is at its peak, you may see those brilliant red sockeyes stacked up like cordwood, finning in 6-inch water.

Moving south down the Peninsula, past the frequently turbid Dog Salmon River, flows the little-frequented King Salmon River (yet another of the five or six King Salmon Rivers in the state), a winding tundra stream that drains Mother Goose Lake into Ugashik Bay. This wilderness flow is as noted for its numbers of bears as for its king salmon fishing, and it also offers good numbers of char, sockeyes, and silver salmon in season.

Slightly south of Mother Goose Lake, flowing through a gorgeous, quaking-aspen-carpeted valley, flows 10-mile-long Painter Creek (the location of Joe Maxey's and Jon Kent's Painter Creek Lodge), part of the Ugashik Bay drainage. This river is noted for its excellent Dolly Varden char fishing and hosts all five species of Pacific salmon.

Some 18 miles farther south flows the Cinder River, a small, mostly shallow, usually clear-running, westerly drainage originating from the black cinder beds of Aniakchak country. It's another of the difficult-to-access Peninsula streams that are best known for their char and numbers of feisty silver salmon. Located here is Gary King, Jr.'s, respected Cinder

River Lodge, which used to cater only to hunters, but now also guides fly fishers.

Of all the landmarks in this impressive, mountain-rimmed region, it's definitely the huge Aniakchak Volcano on the Pacific side of the Peninsula, which last erupted in 1931, that captures a visitor's attention, for where else can a float plane land on a lake *inside* a volcano? The lake, appropriately called Surprise Lake, is a pristine, 6-mile-wide body of water in the huge Aniakchak Crater. The Crater is part of the impressive Aniakchak National Preserve, the ultrascenic origin of the gushing, sometimes-kayaked, Class IV waters of the Aniakchak River. It's exceedingly majestic country, an area of the Alaska Peninsula where several formidable, 3,000-plus-foot lava-formed craters exist, many of them dominating horizons from the surrounding areas.

Fifteen miles to the southwest lies the westerly flowing Meshik River, originating from steep, windy, snow-covered mountains near Aniakchak. The fairly shallow Meshik, wadable in many places, meanders across a big, marshy, grassy tundra valley for some 50 miles before eventually emptying into Port Heiden at Bristol Bay. This fertile char, king, chum, sockeye, and silver salmon fishery isn't frequented very much, partly because of its marshy, difficult-to-access location, but mostly because of geographical distance. However, it's only a matter of time before the fertile Meshik becomes better known.

The Chignik River, which originates at Black and Chignik Lakes, is located some 30 miles southwest of the Meshik and flows easterly to the Pacific side of the Peninsula. It is one of the richest salmon fisheries in the state, featuring one of the most significant sockeye salmon runs on the entire Peninsula. Because of its overall inaccessibility, including a weir, however, the Chignik simply isn't frequented much by sportfishermen, although recently a village native corporation has been talking of constructing a lodge.

The Alaska Peninsula is one amazing, huge, varied piece of fly-fishing real estate. From what I've experienced of it thus far, no other fly-fishing region in Alaska rivals the Peninsula in rugged, untouched, unspoiled beauty. Always bear in mind, however, that it can be a truly unforgiving land, and you will be far better off employing a guide from one of the few sportfishing lodges in the region.

As seen from an airplane, the Alaska Peninsula National Wildlife Refuge appears to be one vast, seemingly endless mix of gnarled, volcanic mountains on the Pacific side, interrupted and interwoven by wide, barren tundras extending all the way to the Bristol Bay side, and cut by myriad crisscrossing tundra creeks and rivers of varying sizes and clarities, many of which—weather permitting—make for superb fishing adventures for hardy fly fishers and their guides. As Gary King, Jr., owner and operator of Wildman Lake Lodge (located just north of Mount Veniaminof between Port Heiden and Port Moller) puts it, "Fishing the Alaska Peninsula is where Alaska sportfishing is still a wilderness adventure."

CHAPTER FOURTEEN

Kenai River Country

SOUTH-CENTRAL ALASKA'S PRODIGIOUS KENAI IS THE STATE'S best-known river. Somehow, whenever anyone speaks of fishing Alaska, the Kenai usually becomes part of the conversation, and for very good reason—it's one amazing body of water.

During the course of the season, the Kenai plays host to six of Alaska's most prized sportfish species. Three salmon species have two distinct runs annually: King (chinook) salmon have a first run occurring in May to June and a second run in July. Sockeye (red) salmon have a first run occurring in late June and a second run in early or mid-July, sometimes extending slightly into August. Silver (coho) salmon have a first run occurring from late August into September and a second run from October into November. Pink (humpy) salmon can also be found there during late July in even years, and there are numbers of trophy rainbow trout and Dolly Varden char from June through October.

Paralleled by steep, magnificent, Dall sheep–inhabited, snowcapped mountains on either side, the upper Kenai River begins at the outlet of the wishbone-shaped Kenai Lake, at the community of Cooper Landing, and meanders some 75 miles in all, passing through 17-mile-long Skilak Lake in the process. It flows westerly across south-central Alaska's Kenai Peninsula before eventually emptying into the frigid waters of Cook Inlet and the Gulf of Alaska. By the time the Kenai eventually enters Cook Inlet (having passed through the waters where the largest strain of king salmon in the world are found), the Kenai definitely qualifies as being big, deep water.

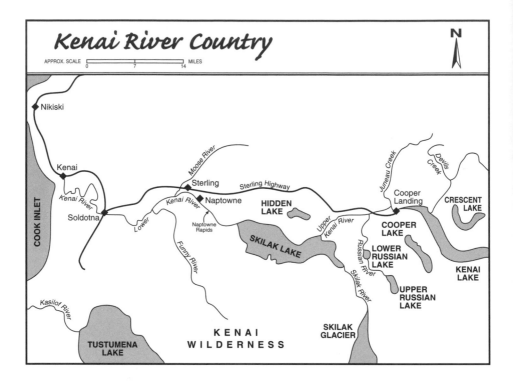

The Kenai is a large river, and over the course of its journey to Cook Inlet, it is such a mix of diverse water that there is no simple means of describing its overall flow, nor can a fly fisher become proficient in the ways of approaching fly-fishing the Kenai without devoting years to learning the river's ever-changing attributes. As many Kenai guides can attest, there are simply too many tributaries and channels of varying depths and water types for any one, all-encompassing description of how to go about approaching the Kenai.

Many first-time Kenai fly fishers soon learn that employing the services of an experienced, professional Kenai River guide (guide services can be found along the Sterling Highway near metropolitan areas) is worth every penny. Experienced Kenai guides know which channels of the river to fish, where to get out and fish from banks and islands, what fly lines and flies to use, where to locate salmon holding and resting waters, and where to hunt for trophy rainbows and Dolly Varden.

Basically speaking, for the fly fisher's purposes, the Kenai River can be divided into two main sections: the upper Kenai and the lower Kenai. Both of these sections vary greatly, offering several diverse fly-fishing challenges. Both sections are easily accessible by boat or automobile at a number of access points along the Kenai's flow, including gravel and dirt roads, trails, and pulloffs. The communities of Cooper Landing, Sterling, Soldotna, and Kenai offer the river's major access points.

THE UPPER KENAI

In spite of the numbers of anglers you will encounter there, the upper Kenai is a world-class trout, salmon, and char fishery. This is the preferred section of the river for fly fishing and is officially designated a trophy trout and char area. The upper Kenai begins at Kenai Lake and flows for some 18 miles through mountains and forests to the frigid waters of 700-foot-deep Skilak Lake. A typical raft or drift boat journey along the upper Kenai will take the fly fisher past the confluence with the Russian River, past the state-operated ferry, and down 4 miles to Jim's Landing, an often-used take-out point. From there the Kenai constricts, careening through a remote, 7-mile stretch of Class II and III water commonly referred to as the Canyon, and eventually emptying into Skilak Lake.

During the course of its flow, the aqua blue Kenai River varies from about 60 to 130 yards in width, and from knee-deep water in places to many 15-foot or deeper holes and runs, offering the angler a wide assortment of water types and fly-fishing challenges.

Although there are several areas of the upper Kenai River where prime salmon fishing does exist, many fly fishers basically look at the upper Kenai as being trophy rainbow and Dolly Varden water. For the past several seasons, because of spawning areas that exist along the river, the entire upper Kenai has been closed to king salmon fishing, and it is closed to *any* form of sportfishing during the spring rainbow trout spawn, from April 15 through June 10. Generally speaking, except for certain salmon holding and resting areas, such as just below Kenai Lake or at the confluence with the clear-flowing Russian River, fly fishers seeking dime-bright salmon action will probably fare better on the lower Kenai, below Skilak Lake.

The waters of the Kenai are a unique turquoise blue, with a distinct, partially silty hue, or glacial tint. This is largely because of a number of small, glacier-fed tributaries that, combined with a handful of clear-running streams, come together to form the scenic Kenai Lake and, subsequently, the Kenai River. But despite the river's siltiness, fish can see well enough through the somewhat murky waters to quickly attack many of the loose, bouncing, natural-drifting food items that happen by.

Although the upper Kenai definitely qualifies as being *big* water (particularly at its outlet, just below Kenai Lake), it isn't nearly the large flow that it will become as it continues its long, meandering seaward journey. The upper Kenai widens out and braids off into several broken channels here and there along its course (which roughly parallels the Sterling Highway all the way to the community of Kenai), offering fly fishers many good, accessible locations, including various islands and several long, broad, rocky beaches, where a fly fisher may get out of the raft or drift boat and probe the Kenai's currents by foot or from its banks.

One of the hottest spots for salmon and rainbows along the upper Kenai is where the popular Russian River intersects it, a confluence that offers fly fishers one of Alaska's premier angling opportunities. Especially during mid-July, when legions of sockeye salmon arrive, there are often several hundred anglers standing fairly shoulder to shoulder, probing the waters, fishing any number of fly configurations, even via spinning rods. As the popularity of the Kenai continues to grow, this has become the norm for this popular roadside fishery.

For the most part, fly-fishing the upper Kenai is best accomplished by drifting from a drift boat or an inflatable raft, as the water is frequently too deep and too swift to wade, although there are several places— islands, rocky beaches, and silt-laden banks—along the course of the upper Kenai where a fly fisher can pull over and fish from the bank or from nearby shallows. The typical procedure is for a fly angler to fish from the boat while it drifts along with the currents until a likely seam, confluence, or island is spotted, there pulling over, securing the boat, and then fishing from the banks or from rocky islands, or wading out into the currents where possible.

Typically, nymphing a single-egg pattern downstream of islands and at drop-offs is effective for rainbows and Dollies, numbers of which are often finning in the currents there, lurking just out of sight, waiting for something that looks edible to appear through the Kenai's semisilty waters. (Note that several 15-pound rainbow trout and Dolly Varden are caught and released in the upper Kenai annually.)

The Canyon, a beautiful, remote, scarcely fished stretch of prime wilderness between Jim's Landing (near the entrance of Upper Skilak Loop Road) and Skilak Lake, is a lovely stretch of trophy rainbow and char water. On a clear day, the region adjacent to the entrance of the Kenai River into Skilak Lake makes for one of the most impressive sights in all of Alaska. Numbers of bald eagles and other wildlife are common, and there are majestic views of the imposing Skilak Glacier and surrounding snowcapped Kenai Mountains. Despite the recent increase in the numbers of rafts frequenting this recreational area of the Kenai Peninsula, the Canyon is still very much wild country, an area where brown bears are sometimes encountered, even though it's within hiking distance of the Sterling Highway.

Although there are areas of the upper Kenai where sinking-tip lines may be used, particularly during late August and September, when pods of silver salmon are frequently found resting in moderate currents during their upstream migrations, in the shallower upper sections of the Kenai, rainbows and Dolly Varden are most successfully taken with floating lines and long, tapered leaders having sufficient split shot attached to simulate a natural downstream drift.

A few weeks after salmon begin to arrive in fresh water, single-egg imitations become the fly of choice, but long, dark leech, sculpin, streamer, and Woolly Bugger imitations can be successful too. (Keep in mind the old adage, "To hook big fish, use a big fly.")

There is often a chop on the upper Kenai's surface as the swift currents travel downstream over large rocks, so it is important to use large, colorful, easily seen strike indicators, attached just where the leader is knotted to the end of the fly line. It's best to use one of the extra-large Kenai River strike indicators, especially when executing a 30- or 40-yard-long downstream drift, so that you can see when a strike occurs. Bob and Curt Trout (of Alaska Troutfitters, located at Cooper Landing), two of the best Kenai guides and fly fishers I've ever met, who use these large strike indicators almost to perfection, informed me that when using the downstream loop technique, it's best to execute a swift, upstream, horizontal hook set.

Although the Kenai does experience significant caddis, mayfly, and stonefly hatches from time to time, there are few fly anglers who concentrate much on fishing dry-fly imitations. Given the delay in fishing until mid-June due to the rainbow trout spawn, combined with the scattering of the river's indigenous species with the arrival of the kings and then the sockeyes, as well as the abundance of drifting salmon flesh in the fall, overall river conditions aren't viewed as entirely ideal for the fishing of dry flies.

Amazingly, most of the upper Kenai River remains ice-free during Alaska's frigid winters, despite frequent subzero temperatures, making certain areas, such as just below Kenai Lake, superb silver salmon and char fisheries on into January and February.

THE LOWER KENAI

From the extremely deep, frigid, and fertile waters at the outlet of Skilak Lake, and for a distance of some 50 miles downstream to the salt waters of Cook Inlet at the Gulf of Alaska, the lower Kenai offers widely varied fishing opportunities for both floating and sinking-tip lines. This section of the river is in places very deep and often swift, and in other places moderate and meandering.

The 17-mile-long Skilak Lake serves as a midway sanctuary for salmon migrating upstream, and consequently, the outlet of Skilak becomes a virtual spillway for abundant quantities of loose, drifting salmon eggs and salmon flesh amid the downstream wash. Not coincidentally, the 2 or 3 miles of deep water just below Skilak Lake have produced some of Alaska's largest sportfish trophies.

Many of the seemingly insignificant seams and confluences found in the lower section of the river produce some of the Kenai's best fishing, not to mention some of the largest fish, so be sure to watch for and fish confluences with smaller adjoining streams, such as the Moose River at Sterling and the Killey River.

Although there are no absolutes when it comes to fishing the Kenai, generally speaking, the lower section is often considered the river's prime salmon water. Several deep holes and runs exist, many of them in the upper portion of the lower river. Fewer boats are seen in this middle portion of the Kenai, making it an attractive alternative to more crowded areas of the flow. The Great Alaska Fish Camp, located where the Moose River joins the Kenai, is an excellent lodge on this less frequented portion of the middle Kenai.

The period just around July 4 often marks the beginning of the second (and larger) sockeye salmon run, although it's those first-run sockeyes, which typically enter the Kenai during mid-June, that often ignite the attention of resident and nonresident anglers alike.

Mint-bright sockeyes, or bluebacks, always migrate fairly close to the banks when making their upstream journeys. This plus for fly fishers is negated somewhat by the fact that while at sea, sockeyes survive primarily on plankton, making them the most difficult of Alaska's salmon species to entice to a fly, despite their close proximity to riverbanks. In calm water, they often will not strike at flies. In moderately swift, moving water, however, and particularly when they are working their way upstream, they have the habit of nipping at flies, especially those that drift directly into their line of vision. It's almost as if they become irritated with any obstructions in their migration upstream. Sockeyes, and kings as well, often hook themselves while nipping at the fly. So be sure to fish moderately flowing seams and confluences.

As soon as you see or feel your line begin to tighten, raise the rod, set the hook, and clear the fly line to the reel as quickly as possible, for pound for pound and inch for inch, these dime-bright, fresh-from-the-ocean sockeye salmon apply the most "horsepower" of all of Alaska's salmon at the end of a line.

Now the battle is on, and often you'll have to scramble downstream with the irate sockeye as it hurries into deeper, swifter currents in search of safety. At this point in the battle, having adequate tippet strength (usually something in the 0X category), a stout 8- or 9-weight fly rod with sufficient butt strength, and a reel with a fairly stout drag will aid your chances of eventually landing a fish.

The lower portion of the Kenai, from the Soldotna Bridge to the Kenai's lower mouth at Cook Inlet, is where most of the Kenai's largest king salmon are encountered. Because the Kenai's kings are the largest strain of chinook salmon in the world, this portion of the lower river attracts hordes of anglers from around the globe. Large numbers of serious gear anglers concentrate their fishing efforts here, and this big, deep water is not generally considered to be fly-fishing water. One of the most common means of gear-fishing this portion of the lower Kenai is to back-troll large gear through deep eddies and runs. During king season, hundreds of gear fishermen frequently use this technique, and sometimes there are so many boats that traffic jams actually occur, making casting a fly line all but impossible.

Sportfishermen and commercial fishermen are frequently at odds with one another over *who* gets what percentage of *what* of the Kenai's incoming Pacific salmon, and Alaska Fish & Game officials will soon be placing added restrictions on fishing the Kenai. If possible, when fishing the Kenai, try fishing during the middle of the week, when there likely will be fewer other anglers.

On May 17, 1985, Les Anderson of Soldotna managed the world's record sport-caught Alaska king salmon—a 97.4-pounder—while gear-fishing near the confluence called Honeymoon Cove. Today, anglers can view this beautifully mounted reproduction at the Kenai Visitors Center. The tremendous girth of this impressive trophy is truly amazing.

Just as occurs at several of Alaska's other flows, the Kenai's indigenous rainbow trout and sea-run Dolly Varden base much of their existence on the return of the various salmon species each year. They begin following the various salmon species upstream during the salmon's spawning migrations, vacating their deep haunts in lakes in search of those hundreds of thousands of nutritious, drifting salmon eggs. During fall, decaying flesh from the dead salmon carcasses makes up a large part of the rainbows' and Dollies' diet. At this time of the season, flesh patterns work best for attracting these fish.

OTHER KENAI PENINSULA FISHERIES

There are other, somewhat smaller streams and rivers of importance to the fly fisher on the Kenai Peninsula. (*Note:* Be mindful to respect private property when fishing in these areas.) The outlet of the huge Tustumena Lake, for example, a fairly sizable flow called the Kasilof River, is easily one of the best spring steelhead opportunities awaiting the drive-to fly fisher. The Kasilof is one of the first rivers on the Kenai Peninsula to get a good, strong run of king salmon, and in July, the Kasilof frequently plays host to an impressive sockeye salmon run. Good Dolly Varden fishing can also be found nearly anytime on the Kasilof, which is easily accessible and only an hour and a quarter south of Cooper Landing.

Only a few minutes farther south is Crooked Creek, a fairly small, shallow stream that is highly frequented by both locals and nonresidents. Crooked Creek, which features a fair amount of alders and some tough-to-get-to fishing, eventually drains into the Kasilof. It offers good spring and fair fall steelhead runs, and Dolly Varden are plentiful.

Fall-fishery Kenai Peninsula steelhead rivers include the Ninilchik River, Deep Creek, and the Anchor River. The Ninilchik is not easily accessible and is probably the least-fished river on the peninsula. The Ninilchik offers fly fishing for kings, Dollies, and fall steelhead, as well as a fairly good silver salmon run. Some of the best water lies 3 or 4 miles upstream of the highway.

Deep Creek has a fairly substantial king salmon run and thus receives more than its share of fishing pressure at times. After the king salmon fishing, however, the pressure diminishes, and any fly fisher ready to brave a few overhangs, willows, and alders and press upstream is likely to find some excellent Dolly Varden fishing. Come late August, silvers and steelhead begin running, and to many fly fishers, this is the best time of year to visit the upper waters of this wadable creek.

The lovely, panoramic Anchor River holds some very special memories for me, for it was here—on my second cast—that I hooked my first steelhead. Today the Anchor continues to receive a growing amount of fishing pressure, both from the local community and from fly fishers traveling down the Kenai Peninsula from Alaska's larger metropolitan areas.

If you want to experience the Anchor's steelhead, silver, and Dolly sweetness, I suggest you avoid weekends, fish early in the morning or later in the evening, check out the tide tables for optimum tides and runs, and fish later in the fall season when the numbers of anglers decrease somewhat.

KENAI PENINSULA LAKES

Higher up in the mountains paralleling the Kenai Peninsula exist several worthy lakes, most of which feature outstanding scenery and good fishing for rainbows, Dollies, or arctic grayling, depending upon the time of year. These include Ptarmigan, Crescent, Johnson, Cooper, Upper Russian and Lower Russian, and Swan Lakes. Much of the best fishing is found at the lake inlets or outlets. Some of these lakes are accessible by roads or trails, but for others, float planes might be the best means of access. Several offer excellent opportunities for float tube fishing.

CHAPTER FIFTEEN

Kodiak Island
and Southeast Alaska

NO OVERVIEW OF ALASKA'S MOST ENTICING RIVERS WOULD be complete without Kodiak Island's Karluk River, flowing to the northwest shores of the island, and the lovely little Situk River, 9 miles from the town of Yakutat, on Alaska's southeastern Panhandle. Both of these rivers rank among Alaska's top salmon, trout, char, and steelhead waters and have earned high marks with fly fishers.

KODIAK ISLAND

The Karluk River is a 22-mile flow originating at pristine, mountain-surrounded Karluk Lake and flowing northward to the salt waters of Shelikof Strait. The Karluk, part of the vast Kodiak National Wildlife Refuge, is located some 70 miles southwest of the city of Kodiak, and there are only local trails in the area, so it is accessible only by boat or aircraft. If you want to fish the Karluk, you have several options: You can fly from Kodiak via float plane to the headwaters of Karluk Lake; fish at a midriver access called Portage, which can be reached by making a 3-mile portage across the tundra after arriving at Larsen Bay or by float-planing to Portage itself; get dropped off at Karluk Landing Strip, at the lower mouth of the river, via wheeled aircraft; or travel to the lower mouth of the Karluk via float plane at Karluk Lagoon. Some commercial outfits also use helicopters to access points along the river.

The Karluk is outstanding not only for its numbers of fish species (king, red, chum, pink, and silver salmon, as well as Dolly Vardens, steelhead, and indigenous freshwater rainbows), but also for its vast wadability. It is a fly fisher's delight, wide and open, fairly shallow in many places, and usually very clear.

Some fly fishers, at certain times of the season, have experienced fifty- and sixty-fish days. And it's common for a fly fisher to be out after one kind of fish and discover large numbers of other species as well.

With Kodiak's typical strong runs of king salmon beginning in early June, a trip to the Karluk is often the kickoff to a fly fisher's annual Alaska fishing agenda, as well as a high point. Even though king salmon fishing on the Karluk doesn't peak until mid-June most years, there are usually decent enough numbers of 15- to 30-pounders during the early part of the month to warrant serious attention.

In August and September, numbers of silver (coho) salmon begin running in fairly amazing numbers, making the fishing again spectacular. If you can wait until *late* September, not only are silver salmon likely to be present in substantial numbers, but you'll also have a good chance of encountering a fall run of Karluk steelhead. Come October, steelhead fly fishing only improves. The Karluk also offers good freshwater rainbow fishing, most which is found from the Portage area upstream to Karluk Lake.

The Karluk is tidally influenced, and optimum fishing often depends on incoming tides. During low-water periods, don't overlook the possibility of "sight fishing," or hunting individual fish, particularly kings.

Some native groups have begun charging land-use fees for fishing the Karluk, anything from $75 to $150 per day per individual or per tent. Also note that camping spots are not abundant at the Karluk, and only a handful of public cabins are available for rent.

Alaska brown bears are commonly encountered at the Karluk, and many anglers carry 12-gauge shotguns or large-caliber sidearms, if only as a precautionary measure.

The smaller Ayakulik River is often regarded as second-best of Kodiak's fly-fishing rivers. Located 80-some miles southwest of Kodiak and about 320 miles southwest of Anchorage, this river is accessible only by float plane. The Ayakulik, also called the Red River, is well known for its early-June king salmon run, superb September silver salmon fishing, and October through November steelhead run. During the summer months, red and pink salmon are abundant, as are numbers of Dolly Varden. Drop-offs are initiated where currents are wide and deep enough to accommodate float planes, usually near the outlet of Red Lake or near the confluence of Bear Creek.

The Dog Salmon, or Frazer, River is another attractive Kodiak Island flow. It has few steelhead, and king salmon fishing is currently prohibited, but there are strong runs of red, pink, and silver salmon, as well as Kodiak's prime chum salmon fishing, and the numbers of Dolly Varden

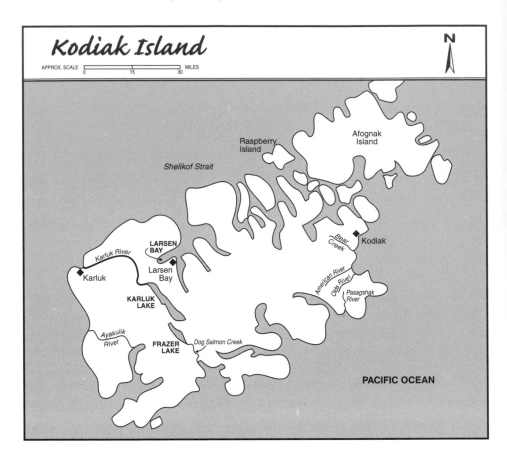

char can be astounding. There is a falls about a mile and a half down-stream of Frazer Lake, so fly fishers usually fish at the upper section, just below Frazer Lake, or down near the mouth, at a spot called Dog Salmon Flats, where the Frazer divides and flows into Olga Bay. Note that bears are abundant around the Frazer.

There are several other, fairly attractive drive-to flows on Kodiak Island for the fly fisher to consider, several of which are accessible from the Chiniak Road (which can be accessed by automobile from the town of Kodiak), at varying milepost markers. These include the Buskin, American, Olds, Chiniak, and Pasagshak Rivers, and Sargent Creek.

SOUTHEAST ALASKA

Southeast Alaska's Situk River, another world-famous, tidally influenced flow, is accessible via a 9-mile road originating in the town of Yakutat.

Compared with many of Alaska's other highly esteemed rivers, the Situk is a fairly small flow. In the course of its 20-mile meander through the dense Tongass National Forest, the Situk is brushy in many places, and sweepers and logjams are common.

The Situk is probably best known for its numbers of spring- and fall-run steelhead, but it also has strong runs of king, red, chum, pink, and silver salmon, as well as Dolly Varden char and a smattering of cutthroat trout. (Unlike some other nearby streams in southeast Alaska, sea-run cutthroat trout are not prevalent in the Situk, although an occasional cutthroat shows up every once in a while.)

There's a little-used aircraft landing strip near the eastern bank of the river, but because of the surrounding forest, it's extremely difficult to find it and to access the river from the strip. Most fly fishers who visit the Situk River fly commercially to Yakutat, secure a room at a hotel or bed-and-breakfast, and fish the Situk on a day-to-day drift basis, under the expertise of a local guide.

Some people prefer fishing the Situk with a floating line rigged with a long leader and split shot, while others prefer a sinking-tip line.

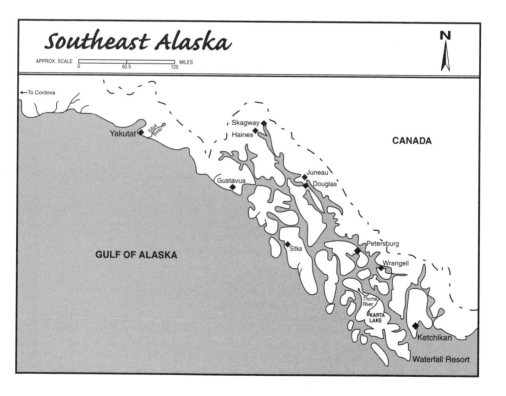

"Even though the Situk is a fairly small river," an experienced guide told me, "fishing it can be a bit difficult at times. The Situk's flow is quite a bit quicker than many realize at first, and along the river's course there are several long, fairly deep holes and runs to challenge the angler. Much of the Situk's fishing is done via wading, rather than fishing from banks, but there are very few gravel bars and islands on which a fly fisher may stand and cast."

He also informed me that some of the Situk's steelies can grow to be as large as 44 inches and weigh up to 25 pounds, although typical Situk fish average about 33 inches and 12 pounds.

The best times for fishing for Situk steelhead are typically from April 1 (or when the river becomes accessible) through the third week of May, and then again in the fall, from the third week in August until mid-October, or until conditions preclude access to the river. Due to overwintering, numbers of spring steelhead are usually superior to those in the fall.

As great as it can be at times, the Situk faces some problems. Recently, some property heirs were awarded custody of a long-standing land claim settlement, making several acres of prime lower Situk property officially off-limits. This just happens to include the spot where drifters have typically exited the river. Fly fishers may still access the Situk up at the old "9-Mile" concrete bridge and there begin the usual 14-mile downstream drift to the lower mouth, but as this is written, anglers are not legally able to exit the Situk at the original outlet. The only problem is that there *are* no other choices for exiting the lower Situk, other than by boat (since there is only one road that leads anglers back to the town of Yakutat), and this makes one wonder what effects outboard motors might have on the river and its fishing.

Fortunately for fly fishers, there are several other attractive flows in southeast Alaska. Fact is, there are approximately sixty other, little-known, little-explored, little-fished streams and rivers in southeast Alaska, offering everything from superb silver salmon fishing to very good cutthroat trout fishing, as well as numbers of steelhead in many of them.

From the air, southeast Alaska appears to be an endless array of picturesque saltwater coves and bays bordered by the dense, coastal blankets of Sitka spruce and hemlocks of the Tongass National Forest, much of which is crisscrossed by countless streams and creeks that eventually meander to the salt waters of the Gulf of Alaska. Southeast Alaska is record rainfall country, so don't forget your rain jacket. Temperatures are typically fairly moderate, especially in the northernmost regions of the southeast Panhandle, with mild winters and cool summers, making for a delightful environment for fly fishers wishing to experience this lush, scenic region of the state.

Ketchikan is a primary corridor to another of southeast Alaska's gems, Prince of Wales Island, the third-largest island in the United States (behind Kodiak Island, which is second only to Hawaii). This island is one of Alaska's best-kept fly-fishing secrets, with large runs of steelhead, numbers of mint-bright silver salmon and sea-run Dollies, and various opportunities at sea-run cutthroats.

Of the several streams on Prince of Wales Island offering good fly fishing, the most productive and highly regarded is the Thorne River, on the island's northeast shore, which flows some 8 miles from Thorne Lake to the salt water of Thorne Bay. The Thorne River offers excellent numbers of steelhead, chums, pinks, silvers, Dolly Varden, and sea-run cutthroats, in season. The highly regarded Boardwalk Lodge is located nearby.

On the southwest shores of Prince of Wales Island, located at Punta San Antonio, is Waterfall Resort, an expansive, beautifully refurbished cannery that has been converted into a world-class fishing resort, located in one of the most scenic fishing areas in southeast Alaska. With its many nearby saltwater coves and bays, the Waterfall Resort region of the island has large numbers of whales, seals, porpoises, and powerful, mint-bright Pacific salmon. Dozens of bald eagles are frequently seen gliding over-head, riding lofty breezes. Anglers can fish from boats, probing the ocean bottom for halibut, rockfish, or lingcod, or cast flies or gear to bright king and silver salmon.

There are many other Prince of Wales Island flows to consider, including the Karta, the Klawock, and the Sarkar. Prince of Wales Island has hundreds of miles of logging roads crisscrossing it in every direction, and many of them lead to some of the most undisturbed flows in the southeast. These can make grand destinations for adventurous salmon, Dolly Varden, and steelhead fly fishers.

One problem with exploring these remote Panhandle rivers, how-ever, is that it can be difficult to get to many of them. Hiring a float plane or wheel plane (depending on the final destination) and flying out from Cordova, Petersburg, Juneau, or Ketchikan is the best means of accessing many of these little-visited streams. Before traveling to any of these entic-ing fisheries, it's important to check with knowledgeable individuals and state and local agencies regarding the best times for making trips, taking into consideration seasons and particular runs.

PART FOUR

The Fish
and the Fishing

CHAPTER SIXTEEN

Catch and Release

 THE GROWING PRACTICE OF CATCH AND RELEASE MAKES A lot of sense. As the majority of fly fishers have come to learn, if we kill a fish, we can't enjoy catching it a second time, and we're removing a fish that likely would have produced many offspring (a hen rainbow, for example, averages some three thousand eggs annually). And a fish swimming away is a far prettier sight than a dead one.

Dwindling numbers of the various sportfish species over the past couple of decades have taught us the importance of releasing fish, and Alaska's fishing lodge owners are helping to lead the way in educating anglers against the killing of indigenous species, including rainbow trout in particular, as well as limiting the killing of Alaska's five species of Pacific salmon. Contrary to what some people think, Alaska's seemingly never-ending supplies of fish are, in fact, very much subject to depletion. Let's not forget that the reason why many anglers from the Lower 48 travel to the Great Land today is that in many cases, fishermen have pretty well killed off most of the fish back home. Therefore, today in Alaska, as elsewhere, it is critical that anglers adopt the practice of catch and release and become familiar with the basic techniques of releasing fish unharmed.

When removing a barbed hook, carefully grasp the shank of the hook (taking care not to hold the fish too firmly with the other hand) and press down, away from the barb slightly, and then quickly back out the hook. Forceps or hemostats, with their long pointed noses, accomplish this much better than regular pliers. Forceps also are excellent tools for crimping down barbs before using the hooks. Studies have shown that a crimped barb doesn't just fish as well as a hook having a barb, but it actually penetrates deeper.

Before you release a fish, make sure it is taking in water through the gills for at least a full minute or two. Facing a fish into the currents helps in reviving it. You will know when a fish has regained enough of its strength to be released. Don't rush the release process, but gently hold the fish in the currents, allowing it plenty of time to regain its breathing rhythm before releasing it back into its natural habitat.

Here is how world-traveled fly fisher Randall Kaufmann, co-owner of Kaufmann's Streamborn Fly Fishing Shops in Washington and Oregon, describes "How to Best Land and Release Fish." I don't think anyone has said it better.

Do Not release a tired fish until it has completely recovered. Firmly hold a played-out fish by the tail with one hand and GENTLY SUPPORT the fish from underneath just behind the head with your other hand. Face the fish upstream in an upright position in fairly calm water, but where there is enough oxygen to allow the fish to breathe easily. By moving the fish back and forth in this position the gills will begin pumping life giving oxygen into its system, while at the same time allowing the fish to rest and regain strength lost during the battle. Fish being revived in this manner will often attempt to escape BEFORE they are completely recovered. A good rule of thumb is not to let the fish swim away the first time it attempts to. When fish are released prematurely they will often swim out of sight, lose their equilibrium, turn onto their side and die. It doesn't hurt to revive fish longer than you feel is necessary. This will insure a complete recovery without complications. This process usually takes a minute or two, but fish that are extremely tired can require several minutes. This is especially true preceding, during, and after spawning periods. When you do release a fish, do so in calm water, allowing the fish to swim into the currents at its leisure.

After releasing a fish, move slowly, for any sudden movements may spook fish prematurely. NEVER TOSS FISH back into the water. If you wish to take a photo, try and have everything "set-up" beforehand, before you remove the fish from the water. Cradle the fish carefully, and lift it just slightly above the water so, if it should happen to slip and fall, it will not crash onto hard earth. Fish can also be laid on wet grass for a couple of seconds. Do not put undo strain on the fish by lifting it high or in an unnatural position. NEVER PUT YOUR FINGERS IN THEIR GILLS for this is like puncturing a lung. NEVER SQUEEZE fish as vital organs are easily damaged. Fish will seldom struggle when handled gently. A quick, harmless way to measure fish is to tape off measurements on your rod or buy a "fish tape" which adheres to your rod. Simply slide the rod alongside the fish in the water and you get an accurate measurement. Spring scales are deadly on fish and should only be used for hoisting a net with the fish inside. It is easy to estimate the weight by the length and condition of the fish. The important consideration is to release the fish quickly and unharmed. A fish which is bleeding slightly will probably survive just fine. Even a fish that is bleeding profusely can usually be revived if you are patient enough.

Try to land fish in a reasonable amount of time. The longer some fish are played the more lactic acid builds up in the bloodstream and the more difficult it becomes to revive such fish. Most fatal damage occurs to fish through improper handling, not during the actual hooking and playing of fish. It is best not to handle or remove fish from the water. When a fish is removed from the water it begins to suffocate immediately and the risk is great that it will flop about on the bank, slip from your grasp, or that you may unknowingly injure it or literally squeeze it to death. If you MUST handle fish, be certain your hands are wet, for wet hands will not destroy the protective mucous film on fish, especially trout.

To remove the hook, gently grip the fish by the tail or jaw with one hand, removing the hook with the other. If you are wading, both hands can be freed by slipping the rod into your waders. If a fish is hooked really deep the hook can often be removed with the aid of a long-nosed pliers or forceps. If not, it is best to cut the leader, leaving the fly in the fish. Nature supplies a built-in mechanism which will dissolve the hook in a matter of days. Oftentimes a friend can lend a hand in unhooking and reviving tired fish.

A barbless hook will help insure safe handling and facilitate a quick release. You seldom have to touch the fish as barbless hooks can usually be backed out very quickly using only one hand. Under specific conditions, a net, if used properly, can be a tremendous advantage, allowing you to quickly land and release fish. A net can alleviate fish flopping and thrashing over rocks in shallow water and can greatly aid you in landing a fish when you are waist deep in water. Be careful fish do not become entangled in the net.

By practicing catch and release, you will not only be preserving a resource, but you will also experience a very positive feeling that will add to your enjoyment of fly fishing.

CHAPTER SEVENTEEN

Rainbow Trout

LIKE MANY OTHER AFICIONADOS OF THE LONG ROD WHO spend a fair amount of time wandering, and dreaming about wandering, around the Great Land, somehow I simply associate fishing Alaska with fly fishing for Alaska's rainbow trout. Truth is, chasing *Oncorhynchus mykiss* (no longer *Salmo gairdneri*) around with a fly is largely why some of us choose to make our homes in the frigid North.

Yes, there are times when we desire to feel the tug of Alaska's colorful arctic char, just as a handful of us sometimes feel the urge to flutter tiny dry flies to delightful arctic grayling, and there are times when steelhead and silver salmon will occupy our thoughts. And yes, there are also those cold winter days when many Alaskan fly fishers find themselves dreaming of chasing wily bonefish and permit around sun-drenched saltwater flats. For a good percentage of Alaskan fly fishers, however, it's Alaska's heavily spotted rainbow trout that pretty well keep us going. Whenever I leave Anchorage on yet another Alaska fly-fishing adventure, it's the leopard rainbows I'm usually pursuing, and like many confirmed rainbow addicts, I often find myself daydreaming of trophy and other rainbows I've had the pleasure of catching over the years. Frequently, just hearing the name of a certain river can cause a fly fisher to think back to a certain day when a certain rainbow took a certain fly in a certain manner. Alaska's rainbows have a way of forming indelible memories.

The whole of Alaska's rainbow trout region is located in the bottom one-third of the state. Consequently, if you want rainbows on your Alaska fishing agenda, schedule your trip with a lodge or service located in Alaska's southern regions, within or near the area referred to as the Bristol Bay sportfishing region.

Like the majority of Alaska fly fishers, I've hooked many rainbows on single-egg patterns drifted below schools of milling salmon. A smaller number of fish have been fooled by large, hairy-looking drys floated along the surface of gin-clear Alaska rivers. Like most fly fishers, however, when fishing deep-water situations, I've tended to rely largely on big, bulky streamers—patterns such as a size 2 Egg-Sucking Leech, perhaps, or sometimes a big, ginger-and-orange-colored Flesh Fly. Often a black-and-purple sculpin pattern works well in enticing some of those dramatic, hard-hitting takes fly fishers dream of. These flies, as well as a black Electric Leech, have provided some line-jarring strikes and some memorable fish.

The state record rainbow trout is officially listed as being a 42-pound, 3-ounce fish taken in 1970 off Bell Island in southeast Alaska, likely a very mature, very well-fed saltwater steelhead. Despite the good fortunes of a few, however, hooking and landing a 30-inch or larger rainbow is *not* an everyday experience for Alaska fly fishers. Truth is, managing a 30-inch rainbow in Alaska is fairly akin to managing a 22-incher in the western region of the Lower 48. Only about one in a thousand fly fishers—nationwide—ever gets the opportunity of hooking a rainbow trout that weighs 10 pounds or more, and those memories of special rainbows taken on a fly, those fish that have weighed an honest 8 to 10 pounds or more—a fair percentage of them taken on drys—can be enough to sustain a north-country fly fisher through a long, cold winter.

At the outlet of famed Iliamna Lake, at that big, deep, extra-wide flow called the Kvichak, a fly fisher stands a pretty decent chance of hooking a rainbow trout weighing up to 18 or 20 pounds. I could hardly believe my eyes the day an Iliamna lodge owner hoisted a 37-inch rainbow trout from his freezer, holding it up for me to observe. Seems an angler from out of state had only recently hooked the monster and couldn't bring himself to release it, so the mammoth fish ended up in the lodge freezer. That rainbow must have weighed something close to 18 pounds when caught.

The Kvichak River is considered by many knowledgeable fly fishers to be *the* Alaska river for producing some of the largest rainbows in the state, but there are several other streams in the Bristol Bay area that, at the right time of year, also hold some extremely large rainbows.

For years, Kukaklek and Novianuk Lakes have been considered among Alaska's best locales for producing trophy rainbows. And downstream some, the Alagnak (or Branch) River is another premier rainbow fishery that can be a virtual rainbow heaven at times, a flow where giant rainbows can be found by those who've learned how to read water.

It's no secret that the rainbow trout is *the* fish in the eyes of many Alaska fly fishers. Why? Well, for one thing, rainbows don't just jump; they frequently skyrocket from the surface, providing electrifying action. If a fly fisher hasn't experienced the thrill of a large rainbow grabbing his dry fly at the surface and powering 3 feet in the air, flipping and cartwheeling a couple of times, and then plunging back into the currents, he has missed one of Alaska's premier fly-fishing experiences. Hooking, playing, and releasing Alaska's "hot-blooded" rainbows is a thrill most fly fishers never tire of.

A couple of years ago, John Gierach, author and editor at large of *Fly Rod & Reel* magazine, joined me in Alaska for a ten-day junket. One of the first rainbows John hooked was a 6-pounder that he managed on a dry fly (a size 14 olive Stimulator, if I remember correctly) while we were fishing one of Iliamna's premier rivers. Even though he'd caught and released hundreds of rainbows in his life, John was grinning like a ten-year-old with his very first fish when that big, spotted predator came up, grabbed his fly, and quickly arched his pretty little 5-weight cane rod, catapulting up through the surface in a head-shaking splash. Not two minutes later, and less than 100 yards downstream, a similar-size rainbow neatly tucked my size 12 Adams Irresistible in the corner of its mouth and began peeling backing from my Hardy as though it wasn't about to stop until it reached the waters of Pedro Bay. Like John, I whooped and hollered as if it was the first fish I'd ever caught.

It can really quicken your pulse when you can actually see those big, heavily spotted mature rainbows, with their wide, dark, British racing green backs and their iridescent, crimson-pinstriped sides, just finning there, sipping naturals at the surface or hovering just below, waiting to snatch yet another salmon egg.

One of my greatest rainbow experiences was that day of days I spent with my good friend Tom Bukowski up on an Alagnak tributary—the day I landed a 28½-inch, 12-pound "football" rainbow hen. I was lucky enough that day to manage nearly a dozen more rainbows ranging from 6 to 10 pounds but this didn't even come close to Tom's success: twenty-some trophies all over 6 pounds. Those rainbows were attacking single-egg patterns, hovering like bandits below the schools of congre-gated sockeyes. Several of those crimson-striped predators were so large they looked like trophy silvers from a distance.

I've also had many more rainbow-fishing adventures in Iliamna country. As anyone who's fished this region can tell you, Iliamna has a way of making a rainbow fly fisher out of a salmon angler in a hurry. It's simple, really: A fly fisher ventures out for sockeyes in the morning, and by the time he stops for lunch, he'll have become an addicted rainbow trout fanatic. Believe me, those abundant 6-, 7-, and 8-pound Iliamna rainbows, with their bright magenta racing stripes, are enough to make a visitor think about relocating to Alaska.

There also are dozens of other rainbow streams in the Great Land that are every bit as good for mammoth rainbows. Take the Kulik, over in Katmai, for example. Just a season ago, a companion and I had barely begun fishing when he shouted over, "Get over here, quick! Big fish!"

"Yeah, sure," I hollered back. "*Every* fish you hook is a big fish."

"No, really, this *is* a big fish," he insisted. "Would you please wade over here for a minute and snap a picture of this hog . . . that is, if I can manage to land it?"

So I did, and when my companion eventually managed the fish to hand, he held up a 27-inch, 9-pound rainbow buck. We hadn't even been fishing for five minutes. Maybe they call the Kulik "Angler's Paradise" for a reason.

Several years ago, during my stay at Bobby DeVito's Branch River Lodge—my first experience on the wonderful Alagnak—a group of guides had gathered down at the dock for some casual chatting and rib-bing after dinner and had invited Dad and me to come down and join them. A couple of guides were still at the fish-cleaning bench, filleting some of the day's salmon catch.

Below them in the currents, the resident rainbows were in a feeding frenzy, gorging on the drifting salmon entrails the guides tossed out. It's the kind of habit local rainbows get into at many lodge sites across Alaska. Multitudes of monster rainbows shot up from the depths, sud-denly appearing at the surface, and viciously attacked the salmon pieces drifting downstream with the currents. The action was so intense that a froth was created on the river's surface.

Fortunately, I just happened to have my old reliable 5-ounce, 8½-foot, 7/8-weight bamboo fly rod nearby. Realizing this might be a good opportunity to try my luck a bit, I methodically began working out some floating line, lengthening out a cast, with but a tiny single-egg pattern attached. I let it just drift out there, and *wham*—a midsize rainbow, about 24 inches and 4½ pounds, grabbed my egg pattern just as my fly line was nearing the end of its arc. Almost before I knew I'd hooked it, that rainbow shot up through the water's surface and hung there suspended, shimmering before us in midair. Then, as we watched in disbelief, the rainbow cartwheeled down and smacked with a gut-wrenching, solid thud—right on the wooden deck!

There the fish remained, motionless, as a hush swept over the entire group. We couldn't believe what we had just witnessed.

I quickly laid down my rod, and Dad and I scrambled over to the rainbow. I gently grasped the fish in my hands and made my way down to the riverbank, where I cradled the still-stunned fish in the cool currents. Amazingly, the rainbow was still alive, but it was definitely dazed and in a state of shock.

It was one of the prettiest rainbows I've ever laid eyes on, a typical Kukaklek-system fish, an Alaskan subspecies that is heavily spotted and frequently seems to have a deep, almost translucent, somewhat iridescent blue-green coloration that is somewhat different from most other rainbows.

The guides who had been standing on the dock scrambled over for a closer look at the stunned rainbow. Slowly at first, the dazed fish began to fin, then its gills began to take in oxygen. For what seemed like a full fifteen minutes, I continued to hold the rainbow in the shallow currents while it regained its strength.

Finally, Dad nodded that the fish appeared ready to be released, so I carefully loosened my grasp. When I did, the spotted beauty swam slowly away, casually at first, and rhythmically, until it eventually gained speed and then disappeared into the Alagnak's depths as though nothing out of the ordinary had happened.

For a moment or two we all just stood there in complete silence, staring down into the river, fairly in disbelief. It was an experience that, for me, gave an entirely new meaning to catch and release.

I'm entirely happy to settle for 3-pounders at the surface on dry flies any day, but for the confirmed trophy rainbow fly fisher who *has* to have fish over 8 pounds, I strongly recommend the following waters for opportunities at Alaska's largest rainbow trout:

Kvichak River: The outlet of Iliamna Lake. Rainbows 5 to 20 pounds, possibly the largest in the state. High-density sinking-tip lines a must for fishing deep water below outlet. Also, fish around islands and submerged islands, using floating lines and weighted single-eggs. The braids of the Kvichak, which are found downstream, are also a good place to find trophies. Kvichak rainbows grow to be 37-plus inches.

Kenai River: Premier Alaska rainbow trout habitat. A steady producer year after year; trophies in the 8- to 17-pound class. Check regulations carefully. "Upper-upper" and "lower-upper" sections of the Kenai generally regarded as best prime rainbow water.

Kenai River below Skilak Lake: Four to 5 miles of deep and extremely deep water holding *big* rainbows. This outlet area produces some exceptionally large fish each year. Special midriver drifts are available via several local and guide services.

Newhalen River: Just below the rapids and down to Iliamna Lake. One of the most productive fisheries in the state and an excellent rainbow bet. *Big* water. Excitement in the form of huge rainbows can happen at the most unexpected times. Drift boats required for reaching largest rainbows. Easy accessibility from nearby Iliamna Airport.

Naknek River: Some of the largest rainbows in Alaska. Large, gaudy streamers (especially black leeches, Egg-Sucking Leeches, and rabbit-fur leeches) are frequently the most successful flies. Watch for terrific, line-jarring strikes, especially on the swing. Deep drifting from boats can also be good at midriver; however, the shallower places found upstream, such as at Rapids Camp and Lake Camp, can provide some exceptional trophy rainbow wade-and-cast opportunities.

Kukaklek-Nonvianuk System: Many believe the vivid, iridescent rainbows found here are among the prettiest in the state. Kulik Lodge is located at the headwaters of this outstanding drainage, and Katmai Lodge at the halfway point on the Alagnak. Premier dry-fly fishing upstream in the Alagnak's braids.

Wood River–Tikchik Lakes–Nushagak Drainage: Some of the prettiest dry-fly water in Alaska. This region is known more for numbers rather than size of its rainbows. Wade and cast dry flies, or fish while drifting downstream via johnboat to lake systems. Farther down the drainage, at the beginnings of the Nushagak River, many of the rainbows are pale yellow and profusely spotted.

Western Alaska Rivers: These include the Togiak, Goodnews, and Kanektok Rivers. The largest rainbow trout I've ever seen was taken at the Goodnews River, even though this flow is best known for its silver salmon and char fishing. The wonderful Kanektok and Togiak are also highly praised rainbow fisheries, both offering an assortment of water types and featuring premier rainbow fishing.

Iliamna's Wild Rivers: These include a number of exceptional medium and small wilderness drainages. Timing is of the utmost importance to fishing success here. Rivers in this area provide fly fishers of any experience level with the ultimate in remote-country fishing experiences. Success requires knowledgeable guides, as well as expert pilots to reach many nearly inaccessible Iliamna locations. These remote, wild rivers and streams can contain some very large rainbows in mid-August through September.

After all is said and done, it likely would be an impossible task for anyone to pick one particular rainbow trout fishery as being superior to all other Alaska waters. Truth is, there are such a great variety of rainbow waters found in Alaska's Bristol Bay, southwestern, and western regions that it would be impractical to call one drainage superior to another.

If optimum-size rainbows were the desired goal, the Kvichak, Newhalen, Alagnak, or Naknek would be a good place to start. Fishing any of these very large flows is probably best accomplished by boat (all are big, deep-water fisheries), although there are several places where an angler can get out and wade here and there, fishing from underwater islands, rocks, or sandbars.

Since rainbows are ever in search of, and following, migrating salmon, timing can be extremely important. Where rainbows might have been located yesterday—or where they happened to be a year ago at the same time—is not necessarily where they will be today. As the predatory rainbows begin to follow schools of arriving salmon on their upstream journeys, numbers of rainbows in any given stream can fluctuate greatly. Another factor is plain ol' luck—being in the right place at the right time. Just because a fly fisher is in Alaska at Fabulous Creek doesn't mean he necessarily will discover easy fishing and lots of big fish. Salmon runs and times of runs can vary, and weather, water levels, and water temperatures all influence fish behavior. Consequently, first-timers soon discover fishing in Alaska still means "hunting," and even though numbers of fish—as well as numbers of big fish—are probably higher in the Great Land than in many other places, the challenges still remain.

CHAPTER EIGHTEEN

Alaska's Steelhead

THERE'S SOMETHING MAGICAL ABOUT HOOKING INTO ONE of Alaska's steelhead, those anadromous rainbow trout that ascend Alaska's rivers from the sea each year. These silver-dollar-bright, fresh-from-the-ocean rainbow trout average 28 inches in length and 9 to 12 pounds, although some can be as large as 44 inches and 25 pounds.

Without question, *Oncorhynchus mykiss* are among the most prestigious trophies any fly rodder could pursue. Steelhead are cold-water creatures that almost always require hardy anglers who are willing to brave the elements to catch them. Some of Alaska's best steelhead fishing occurs in mid-April and into May, but for many anglers, steelhead fly fishing quickly brings to mind memories of vivid fall colors and the chill of autumn air.

Generally speaking, Alaska's steelhead are not as large as some of those found elsewhere, especially in Canada's famed Skeena system, which includes the Babine and Kispiox. In Alaska, a 15-pound steelhead is considered to be a dandy, although 20-pounders do manage to get caught on occasion, many coming from southeast Alaska, near Yakutat. Every once in a while a 25-pounder is taken in southeast Alaska, most coming from the Situk, Thorne, and other nearby rivers located on the huge Prince of Wales Island, across from Ketchikan. The Alaska record steelhead, taken in 1970 off Bell Island in southeast Alaska, weighed a whopping 42 pounds, 3 ounces.

Landing one's first steelhead on a fly rod makes for indelible memories, and I still daydream about my first steelhead experience. It was early September, and I was fishing with Dr. Franklin "Doc" Smith from

118

Illinois, with whom I've shared numerous outdoor experiences over the years. The place was south-central Alaska's Anchor River, a lovely little cottonwood-lined stream located not too far from the end-of-the-road community of Homer.

For years I'd heard tales and watched videos of anglers braving the elements and fishing for hours just to finally hook a steelhead. As a first-timer, I figured I'd have to invest many hours just to get a nibble, much less hook and land a steelhead.

It had taken us about four hours of steady driving to get from Anchorage down to the Anchor, and by the time we arrived, it was mid-afternoon and we were more than anxious to stretch our legs and wet a line. While Doc finished rigging his gear in the parking lot, I made my way over to the river just to have a look-see. I fed fly line through the rod's guides as I scanned the various riffles and seams. Then I reached into my fly box and selected the first single-egg pattern I came to, a flame-colored, size 6 Glo-Bug, and tied it on my tippet as a "searcher" fly. Above the fly, I fastened a couple of 3/0 split shot.

The hole directly in front of me looked fairly decent, so I casually made a cast, plopping the fly and split shot down at the top of a seam, allowing the single-egg pattern to drift naturally through the riffles and down through the good-looking hole. Nothing happened, so I picked up and cast again. By this time Doc was walking over.

Suddenly my fly line tightened. Lifting the rod, I set the hook on my very first steelhead. A microsecond later, I was thick in battle with that 10- or 11-pound "chromer." I'd actually hooked a 30-inch steelhead on my second cast!

That steelie's colors were magnificent, and it made for quite a sight as it glistened in the autumn sun. Its head and back were a dark, metallic, cobalt blue, and its gill plate was a shiny, purplish red. I could see why steelhead are so widely revered as sportfish trophies.

A half hour after I released that steelhead, I landed yet another, nearly a twin to the first fish, this time on a big, ugly, brown-and-black Woolly Bugger.

I've ventured out for steelies on only three or four occasions since that day with Doc. A couple of those trips were near duplicates of my first experience, but on another occasion, my partner and I arrived to learn that we had the river all to ourselves. We also learned we'd arrived to an inch and a half of flowing, slushy ice, which greatly impeded our nymphing efforts. Needless to say, we had made our trip too late in the season.

Steelhead are anadromous, meaning that they migrate and exist in both fresh and salt water as part of their natural life cycle. Most anadromous fish species have a stronger preference for salt water during the major feeding and growth phases of their lives, and steelhead trout definitely fit into this category. Many Dolly Varden char are also anadromous.

Some steelhead enter fresh water in spring, others in autumn, but all of them spawn in spring, just like freshwater rainbows do. It is speculated that steelhead trout were once regular rainbows that somehow developed the ability to survive in both fresh and salt water. Or perhaps freshwater rainbows evolved from saltwater ancestors while steelhead remained in the salt. Others speculate that it had something to do with an ice age. A glacier may have formed, cutting off a group of rainbows from returning to fresh water. Nevertheless, it is said that rainbows and steelhead are identical except for a steelhead's ability to survive in salt water. Because of the ocean's vast food supplies, steelhead frequently grow to much larger sizes than do freshwater rainbows, which must pick from scantier offerings. Steelhead are said to have gotten their name from commercial fishermen, who had a tough time killing them when clubbing them over the heads.

An important factor in hooking steelhead is to fish rivers where steelhead are to be found. When fishing a state the size of Alaska, you have to make up your mind in advance to go to a particular river for a particular species at a particular time.

Alaska has more than its share of excellent steelhead streams, but with a human population geared largely to both a private and a commercial salmon harvest and a guiding network established primarily around the five species of Pacific salmon, steelhead guiding remains a largely untapped service in Alaska. The reason? Many of the better steelhead streams in southeast Alaska and the Peninsula are exceedingly difficult to access, and few guides or outfitters can afford to abandon their lucrative salmon business for the less sought-after and less accessible steelhead.

Consequently, many of Alaska's remote, premier steelhead rivers remain all but unexplored. Prince of Wales Island, for example, has many little-known steelhead streams. The Thorne River, located very near the respected Boardwalk Lodge, and the Karta are two well-known, respected steelhead flows on that island.

Alaska's best-known steelhead fisheries are the Situk River near Yakutat, the Karluk River on Kodiak Island, various streams on Prince of Wales Island, and a handful of Kenai Peninsula flows, located fairly near Homer.

The optimum steelhead fly rod is probably an 8-weight or possibly a light 9-weight, one of today's advanced graphite designs. You'll need extra spools containing both floating *and* sinking-tip lines for your reel to meet the varying water conditions you'll encounter. Some of the most consistent Alaska steelhead patterns are a size 2 or 4 purple Egg-Sucking Leech, a size 2 black, purple, or brown-and-black Woolly Bugger, a size 6 or 8 flame- or champagne-colored Glo-Bug, and any of the series of size 2 or 4 two-egg wet flies, such as the Babine Special or a similar, more recent pattern called the Rajah.

Leader tippets are probably best kept at something around 1X. When fishing sinking-tip lines, use short, 3½- or 4-foot leaders to keep flies from buoying off the bottom; when using a floating line, 10- or 11-foot leaders with split shot or lead wraps attached about 12 inches above the fly generally work well. (Check regional fishing regulations for specifics regarding the placement of split shot.)

Although frequently it's the numbers of fish rather than size that makes Alaska attractive to steelheaders, there's no question about it: Steelhead fishing in the Great Land has a certain magic about it.

CHAPTER NINETEEN

Arctic Grayling

 IN THE OPINIONS OF MANY NORTH-COUNTRY FLY FISHERS, a fly-fishing adventure specifically designed around the arctic grayling is not only enticing, but also downright therapeutic. The arctic grayling is a fairly small, fairly common, freshwater species with a vastly enlarged dorsal fin. Arctic grayling supposedly smell like thyme (they do—I've sniffed them), thus their Latin name, *Thymallus arcticus*. This species is a cousin to the whitefish but typically inhabits very cold, crystal-clear lakes and streams. Grayling frequently take flies at the surface, often on their way back down.

In spite of its fairly drab, grayish background, an arctic grayling can be a striking fish, with its long, flowing dorsal fin and its myriad subtle purples, turquoises, and green-and-gold streaked fins. Arctic grayling are a spectacular freshwater species, seemingly created especially with the dry-fly fisher in mind, and they make for a great species for beginning, intermediate, and experienced fly fishers, alike. What makes them especially fun for the intermediate fly fisher is that they are usually very aggressive fish and not all that difficult to catch.

Grayling usually require only a light rod, a fairly long, medium-fine leader, and a simple dry fly. Dark dry flies work well for Alaska's arctic grayling, but any number of size 14 or 16 drys will take grayling all day long, although every once in a while you might want to change flies just to keep things interesting for the fish.

One of my favorite grayling flies might surprise some anglers. It's a size 12 Griffith's Gnat tied with a peacock body, with a wisp of white or grizzly hackle palmered along the length of the body and the barb pinched down. This simple pattern (along with its close relative, the

Renegade) is absolutely deadly on Alaska's grayling. If you've located decent grayling water and if you switch your fly every once in a while when the fishing begins to get stale, you can catch grayling all day long.

Arctic grayling can be taken in many places across Alaska, with the exceptions of the southeast Panhandle, Kodiak Island, and the Kenai Peninsula. Nome and points east and north are prime, old-country grayling habitat, with several premier grayling waters offering some real giants. The flow between Upper and Lower Ugashik Lakes, at the head of the Alaska Peninsula, is generally considered to be *the* trophy grayling region, but Lake Clark country is also a highly respected region for grayling. I know of one particular stream in that area that is so good that my guide made me swear I'd never divulge its name. The first time I fished there, I took an 18-inch grayling on my first cast—and a 20-inch grayling is said to a trophy of a lifetime.

A couple of years ago, on a char and grayling fly-in trip, a companion and I took a number of 20-inch grayling in the upper Alaska Peninsula area, with one confirmed giant going 21 inches. We didn't have any means of weighing that fish, but we estimated it would easily go around 4 pounds, or something very close to the all-time Alaska record, which is currently a 4-pound, 13-ounce fish taken back in 1981.

If you're a confirmed dry-fly aficionado who hasn't had the opportunity of fishing grayling on a 3- or 4-weight fly rod until your wrist begins to ache and your casting arm begins to feel as though it's ready to drop off, you simply haven't experienced one of the pure joys of Alaska fly fishing.

Generally speaking, arctic grayling are found in icy-cold, crystal-clear water; the clearer and colder, the better, it seems. Sometimes they can be found in silty, glacial runoff flows (likely feasting on a salmon egg extravaganza), but for the most part, grayling seem to seek out only the clearest waters. Many grayling streams are so astonishingly clear that it's often difficult to judge the depth of the water. I don't know how many times I've ventured into what appeared to be 3-foot water only to discover it was more like 5 or, *whoops!*, 6 feet deep.

Locating good grayling water is fairly easy. Moderately flowing riffles are frequently good places to find grayling, and other good grayling lies are located just below islands in clear-running streams, or where slow-joining confluences tumble near cut banks. Looking for a slight chop at the top is probably the best way to describe locating excellent grayling water to a newcomer, but keep in mind that nine times out of ten, just downstream, at those places where slightly swifter currents converge, rainbows are likely to be lurking too. Grayling make great sport fish on their own merits, but at least 10 percent of the time in Alaska, a fly fisher will hook some pretty decent rainbows when he's concentrating on grayling. I don't know how many times I've started out fishing for grayling and found myself casting just slightly farther downstream for rainbows instead. Since rainbows seem to enjoy observing grayling feeding lanes, just 10 or 15 more feet can also mean rainbows.

Since many of Alaska's premier fisheries play host to both species, fly fishers often face a difficult choice: Should they cast for grayling or for rainbows? The lovely Agulowak in the Wood River–Tikchik Lakes region is one such flow.

The first time I visited that lovely area, there were so many fish rising around us that at first I didn't think about whether I was casting to rainbows or grayling. All I knew was that there were so many fish surfacing all around us that I'd better get a fly out there quickly. Just six or seven seconds after I cast, I hooked into an 18-inch grayling with a dorsal fin that looked to be 8 inches long. After hooking a dozen or so that were nearly identical, I calmed down a bit and began concentrating on rainbows.

I've also been to other fine grayling waters in the Ugashik region. One very remote stream with no official name comes to mind—a fairly wide flow down on the Alaska Peninsula where the grayling are so chunky that they look like carp. It's a dry-fly fisher's dream stream, all right, although it's hard to land a float plane anywhere near the place. The area is dotted with numerous lakes, most of which are too small for a float plane such as a Cessna 185 to get into, and a fairly long walk from the lake of access through massive tussocks is necessary to get to the stream. Char often frequent the same water as grayling, and although I took numbers of trophy grayling on size 10 caddis patterns that day, the fish I remember most from that remote stretch of river was a 9-pound, gold-and-silver arctic char whose orange-and-pink spots were striking in both size and color. In fact, many of the streams on the Alaska Peninsula are filled with char so brilliantly colored that they look like artists' renditions of fantasy fish.

The best times to fish for arctic grayling in Alaska are mid-May to mid-June and September to late October, but excellent grayling fishing can also be had during the height of the summer.

Next time you're planning an Alaska fly-fishing trip, consider arranging a fly-out adventure designed especially around arctic grayling. Chances are you'll be flown in to a remote, pristine piece of real estate with a picture-book, crystal-clear stream running through it, with few or no other anglers on its banks—one that you can call your own for an afternoon, at least. And once there, chances are you'll be able to hook and release several of what some fly fishers call the "aristocrat of the North."

CHAPTER TWENTY

Dolly Varden and Arctic Char

IT IS THE OPINION OF THIS ALASKA FLY FISHER THAT THE often-maligned Dolly Varden char, sometimes called goldenfin trout, is one of the noblest fish to inhabit Alaska's waters. This fish is accused by some of consuming too many salmon eggs and being harmful to the survival of salmon, but many Alaska fly fishers, including myself, believe Dolly Varden char should be one of Alaska's most respected sport fish. Like hundreds of other Alaska fly fishers, I've simply enjoyed too many memorable days astream battling these scrappy, twisting fighters *not* to respect them. Dollies are dependable and are fairly predictable, and best of all, they're great fun on a fly rod.

Technically, there are six subspecies of char in Alaska. There are, in fact, an arctic char and a Dolly Varden that are anadromous (they exist in both fresh and salt water) as well as an arctic char and a Dolly Varden that exist entirely in fresh water. Additionally, lake trout and brook trout are both char subspecies. (There is one lake in southeast Alaska that holds a number of brook trout, no matter that they were planted.)

There have been ongoing discussions regarding the differences between Dolly Varden and arctic char, and biologists don't always agree on the best way to differentiate between the two. Some experts believe one can tell the two char apart by the size of the pink-and-orange spots on the fish's sides: The spots on the arctic char are larger than the pupils of its eyes, they say, whereas those on the Dolly Varden are smaller than its pupils. Other experts believe that the best way to distinguish between the two species is to count gill rakers or to compare certain muscles near the fish's stomach. (Somehow I think I'd rather be out fishing than counting gill rakers or performing stomach surgery.)

The arctic char is a gorgeous fish. A just-out-of-the-salt Dolly might be less spotted and less colorful than it will be in a month or two, but it's still striking. And a Dolly in its spawning colors can even rival its colorful cousin, Alaska's beautiful lake trout. Fish in the char family, including lake trout, have strikingly beautiful, white-striped fins. These bright white leading-fin markings can appear all but surreal at times and are especially striking on char in their orangish bronze and deep green spawning colors.

Arctic char and Dollies differ from rainbows and salmon in that char have light spots silhouetted against a dark background, whereas rainbows and salmon have dark spots over a light background. These make char—especially in their vivid mating colors—extremely colorful and easy to distinguish from all other Alaska fish.

The Dolly Varden *(Salvelinus malma)* is more numerous than the arctic char *(Salvelinus alpinus)* and is more widespread. The Dolly Varden occupies the entirety of Alaska's char regions; the arctic char, only the extreme northwest part of the state and from Bristol Bay south, down into the Alaska Peninsula and onto Kodiak and Afognak Islands.

Dollies and arctic char aren't jumpers like the rainbows, but they are good, stout fighters, nonetheless. Char tend to fight deep, twisting and turning when hooked. One of their traits, as they approach to take a fly, is to signal a flash. When the angler sees this happen, or sees the end of his fly line twitching or his strike indicator wiggling, it's time to lift the rod and set the hook.

There's no better time to fish for char than when they follow the salmon upstream during the annual migrations. Dollies are often found in greatest numbers during July, August, and September, depending upon the length and timing of the individual salmon runs and the numbers of loose, drifting salmon eggs present. The best months for fishing for arctic char are June, September, and October, although a few of the northern drainages reach their peaks for char in July.

Ninety percent of the successful fishing for char will be had with a deeply fished wet fly, be it a single-egg pattern, a common wet fly, or a nymph. Char are extremely fast swimmers and can often surprise anglers who are fishing a fly through swift confluences, just as they are quick to intercept a waking dry fly (or fry or smolt imitation) at the surface. The trick to getting char to take at the surface is to intentionally wake the fly by moving it faster than the current as well as moving it *across* the current. Frequently, this is best accomplished while standing in less-than-knee-deep water.

Two of the best flies for char are Iliamna Pinkies, tiny, pink, chenille-wrapped single-egg imitations; and Glo-Bugs, slightly larger, yarn-trimmed single-egg patterns. Other good producers are two-egg patterns such as the famed Babine Special or a similar fly called the Rajah. The old reliable Polar Shrimp also takes more than its share of char.

There are still some fly-fishing traditionalists who continually appeal that naturals (such as Gold-Ribbed Hare's Ear nymphs), should be used for taking Dollies "nobly." My reply to this is that Alaska's Dollies and char obviously key in on salmon eggs, and employing a single-egg pattern is simply Alaska's version of matching the hatch. Unless the fishing occurs before the salmon eggs begin to drift in the currents, during which time a small, brown, wet-fly nymph can be the fly of choice, fly fishing for any type of char is usually best with an egg pattern. There *are* times when fry and smolt patterns are just the ticket for char, however. When fishing early or late in the season or when fishing lake mouths, try tumbling or stripping a smolt pattern and expect good results. Arctic char and Dollies might not exactly be gourmets, but they do know a good deal on a fish dinner when they see one.

Char are usually found lying deep, running at or near stream bottoms. They often look like gray ghosts, barely distinguishable on the stream bottoms. At first it may be difficult to pick out char, but it becomes easier after a bit of practice.

Fly fishing for char in Alaska is often best accomplished with a floating line, a long leader, and a split shot or two crimped about 10 inches up from a single-egg pattern. This way, you can watch the end of your fly line as it floats, while the egg pattern bobs and drifts along in the currents near the bottom in a very natural manner. Call it nymphing, call it boondogging, call it whatever you like, but it sure is fun, and it sure catches char.

It is purported by some that arctic char, on average, tend to weigh more than Dolly Varden, likely because arctic char are often found in more remote, inaccessible, unfished areas. Worldwide statistics seem to uphold that arctic char do average larger than Dollies, although try telling that to a fly fisher who has just managed a 14-pound trophy Dolly Varden! However, most Dolly Varden char found on the Kenai Peninsula average 2 to 5 pounds, and typical char in western Alaska average about the same. The Alaska state record char was a 17-pound,

8-ounce fish taken from the Wulik River where it flows into the Chukchi Sea near Kotzebue.

Both Dollies and char are highly susceptible to mucus disruption by improper human handling. They are more prone than Alaska's other fish species to contracting infections via rough treatment, so be extra-careful when handling and releasing char.

CHAPTER TWENTY-ONE

Lake Trout

LAKE TROUT (*SALVELINUS NAMAYCHUS*), ALSO KNOWN AS mackinaw or lakers, are one of the most beautiful fish of the north country, especially during the fall, when they are in their sensational spawning colors. The dorsal and back are lobster shell green with vermiculated splotches of pale blue; the sides blue-green with tiny spots of silver and gold and dashes of yellow and blue; the belly a rusty-white; and the fins a striking burnt orange, with brilliant white stripes at the leading edges. Yet despite all this color, the lake trout's deeply forked tail is widely considered its most distinguishing characteristic. In contrast to its beautifully colored body, a lake trout's eyes are large, dark, and clear.

The lake trout is not officially a trout at all, but a member of the char family. And like char, the lake trout usually sound deep upon being hooked, often exhibiting a twisting, turning motion during the battle. Unlike rainbows, lake trout don't spend much time aloft.

To a growing number of fly fishers, there's a certain mystique about fly fishing for lake trout in Alaska. Lakers often are found in some of the most isolated wilderness lakes and streams, where they prefer icy, ultra-clear waters. Many of the best lake trout waters of the North are located in pristine wilderness. Lake trout usually make for a challenging and enchanting species on a fly rod, although their battles don't rival a rainbow's, even though their locations often do.

The first laker I ever took on a fly was a solitary "cruiser" whose shadow had been spotted by a member of our party as it roved the waters of a brilliantly clear, pristine backcountry lake. The fish was spotted during our midday lunch break after an exceptional morning of fly fishing for arctic grayling. I was sitting back against a fallen log, munching a sandwich and enjoying the view of the crystal-clear lake and the beautiful, snowcapped mountains reflected on the water's surface.

Suddenly, one of our party hollered out, "Hey, there's a pretty nice laker cruising around out here. Why doesn't somebody come over and see if he can hook it?" The way I saw it, there was nothing to do but put down the other half of my sandwich and have a go at it.

I'd been fishing a pet 9-foot, 5-weight graphite fly rod that morning for grayling. Realizing I'd probably have to go down fairly deep to hook the laker, I hastily unclipped the Griffith's Gnat dry fly I'd been fishing and reached for a weighted Iliamna Pinkie, figuring the bright pink little egg pattern might serve well in attracting the laker's attention. I also added a couple of small split shot about 14 inches up the leader from the fly.

After wading out nearly chest-deep in the clear lake and eventually spotting the fish's cruising shadow on the bottom, I quickly worked out a series of false casts and then executed a fairly long delivery. As luck would have it, I hooked that laker on my first cast! Somehow, I'd managed to lead the moving target just right so as to give the fly time enough to sink and fairly intercept the fish.

I could hardly believe it. Lifting the rod, I snugged the hook past the pinched barb and firmly tightened the line to the rod tip. Five minutes later, after a worthy, but not especially powerful, battle, the beautiful 6- or 7-pound lake trout came to hand. I was more than a bit impressed with its spawning coloration, and I was amazed at the size of its clear, dark eyes. I was also glad I hadn't rushed the fishing experience by "horsing" the laker as it tried to bore down, or sound. I became hooked on lake trout fishing that day.

Since then, I've enjoyed several other experiences with lake trout, although, for some reason, I've never made a fishing trip specifically with lake trout in mind. As with many anglers, lake trout always seem to be a secondary species, often coming as a bit of a surprise, mostly in early summer or late fall, the times of year when lakers will drop down out of the lakes into river mouths to feed on fry, smolt, sculpins, eggs, or salmon flesh. I've even taken lakers on black leech patterns a couple of times.

If I were seriously looking to hook a lake trout, it wouldn't be with a dry fly or even a deeply sunken fly on a lonely lake. Instead, I'd probably opt to fish the inlet or outlet of one of Alaska's fairly large, remote interior lakes, just where the currents converge and begin to riffle quickly.

In the early spring or during fall, places like the outlet of Kukaklek or Naknek Lake, in the Bristol Bay region, can be great lake trout spots, with literally hundreds of the fish. Lake Louise, near Glennallen, also has excellent lake trout fishing.

Lake trout are distributed in two major areas of Alaska: In the north, they can be found in a band reaching from the Beaufort Sea extending southwest to the Kobuk River; in the south, along the entire southern third of the state, extending southwest into the Alaska Peninsula. The Katmai region of the state is an excellent region for lake trout, as are a few scattered westerly regions of the Panhandle.

The remote waters of one of Alaska's Susitna Valley lakes might be a good place for a beginning fly rodder. Try a calm summer evening, perhaps, somewhere around 9 or 10 o'clock, after it's cooled down a bit. Select a lonely, secluded bay or cove, just where a small creek trickles in. Depending upon whether or not you see any activity at the surface, either fish a dry fly at the surface or use a fast-sinking, sinking-tip shooting head and strip a streamer or smolt pattern.

The best times to fly-fish for Alaska's lake trout are June and then when it begins to cool down a bit in September and October. During the hot summer months, lake trout move into the deeper, cooler waters of lakes.

In spring, lakers can effectively be taken on streamers imitating small fish, such as a Blue Smolt, Gray Ghost, or one of the more common, lighter-colored Woolly Bugger tyings, especially one with a touch of Flashabou added. Also consider trying one of the Light Zonker patterns. During spawning time, in the fall, mature males will scurry smolts and smaller fish away from redds (or nests), so employing a streamer is often an effective strategy.

Lake trout often call for cautious, careful fishing, and a wise fisherman will take pains to disturb the natural setting as little as possible. In lakes, you may find lakers on the rise and feeding at or near the surface. This is a wonderful opportunity for exciting laker fishing. Whether you're fishing from a boat, a float tube, or a concealed lakeshore position, you should cautiously work your line out to the appropriate distance and make a delicate presentation using a tiny artificial. If you've tied on a wet fly, streamer, or leech pattern and are fishing a sinking line or a high-density sinking-tip, allow the sinking portion to sink for a few seconds, and then begin retrieving the fly, employing varying lengths of pull and adding erratic, lifelike movements to the fly. If you suddenly feel that you're caught on a snag, chances are you've hooked a lake trout.

Leeches, sculpins, Zonkers, and minnow imitations are all good choices for lakers. Often I've been fishing for rainbows near a lake's outlet with a sinking-tip line rigged with a leech or sculpin imitation, only to be surprised with a nice laker instead.

For lake trout fishing, an 8-weight rod is good for both the casting distance it offers and its wind-bucking capabilities, and the rod should be at least 9 feet long. With a little heavier rod, you can throw larger, weighted flies when required, but dry-fly fishing can be enjoyable too.

The Alaska record lake trout was a behemoth 47-pounder, taken at remote Clarence Lake back in 1970, but the average fly fisher will enjoy a good time hooking lakers weighing around 5 to 8 pounds.

CHAPTER TWENTY-TWO

King of Salmon

OF ALL THE GRAND SPECIES TO BE EXPERIENCED IN ALASKA, the giant king salmon seems to be the one that most excites anglers. Hooking an immense king salmon *(Oncho-rhynchus tshawytscha)*, also known as chinook, blackmouth, tyee, or spring salmon, often is all many anglers dream about for months before their trip.

Even though many anglers should know better and should spend their time dreaming of, and fishing for, Alaska's rainbow trout instead, countless fly fishers from around the world fantasize of nothing other than hooking one or two of Alaska's famed, giant, black-lipped kings. But after having had the dubious pleasure of being dragged around a river—under fallen logs and across beaver dams—by an irate king salmon pulling like an unforgiving freight train at the end of the line, I'm quite happy to state, categorically, "I ain't never fly-fishin' for kings again!"

Why would anyone say a thing like that in a book about fly fishing? Well, as far as I'm concerned, fly fishing for Alaska's king salmon is definitely to be considered a radical sport. Fact is, everybody's out there looking for big fish. It's just that some of us are entirely happy pursuing 12-pound rainbows, whereas others aren't satisfied until they hook and battle a creature the size of a barge.

Granted, there are times when fly fishing for king salmon can be incredible—when water conditions and your timing are just right, when moderate-size kings are stacked up like cordwood—but fly fishing for kings can also prove to be a frustrating business, especially when you can see them but can't, for the life of you, seem to get your fly down to the fish. Not only that, but successful fly fishing for king salmon is always tough on the elbows. As one friend described it, "Battling a king on a fly rod is a lot like arm wrestling with someone who's ten times stronger than you are; every once in a while you might *think* you're beginning to get the advantage, but then, suddenly, the real boss comes to life and shows you who's really in charge."

Yet fly fishing for kings definitely qualifies as being great sport, and there are times when I can see why people are so attracted to fishing for creatures the size of baby grand pianos.

The first *big* king salmon I ever tackled on a long rod was a 45-pounder that dragged me around the river like a wet rag for nearly two hours before I was finally able to beach the thing. For a while there, I thought the king was going to win. Then I decided to get serious and made up my mind to end the battle, once and for all. I dug in my heels and began cranking and pulling for all I was worth, watching my rod tip as well as the movements of the fish, and finally, eventually, my once-in-a-lifetime dream came true.

In the end, as I stood there panting on the riverbank, nearly exhausted, I looked down at the bright chrome monster I'd subdued. Sadly, now, it was still gasping to catch its breath, as was I. By that time I'd already pulled the tops of my neoprene waders halfway down because I was perspiring so. And a minute later, when I glanced down again at my prize, I realized that I had just finished a merciless battle with one of God's most wondrous creatures of the sea. That king salmon was so fresh from the ocean that it still had several sea lice clinging to its sides.

Earlier that morning, Greg Bell, of High Adventure Air service in Soldotna, had flown a companion and me in a deHavilland Beaver across Cook Inlet to a secluded king salmon stream, where we landed on a small, pristine tundra lake and then made a short hike over to a beautiful, clear-flowing river. Amazingly, no other anglers were present. We could hardly believe we had that world-class Alaska river all to ourselves.

Looking back on that trip, my only disappointment is that I killed that dime-bright king. It was early in my fishing career, and the way that king had fought, I reasoned it deserved a place on a wall at the office or, if my wife would allow it, in our home.

However, after returning to the city and learning that it would cost $650 to have that king salmon mounted, I began to feel rather stupid for having killed that giant. Almost as painful had been the effort it had taken my companion and me to lug those 45 pounds of dead king salmon 2 miles back through the spruce forest to the float plane.

Today, I realize that beautiful king salmon deserved better. What it deserved was a gentle release back to freedom and a chance to spawn, to create additional numbers of its kind. But at the time, I hadn't lived in Alaska long, and like many beginners, I was fairly unschooled about the importance of releasing fish. I had yet to learn that the ultimate fishing victory comes *after* subduing a quarry—when a fly fisher releases a fish—so that he can not only experience the honor seeing his trophy swim back to freedom, but also recognize that by releasing fish, he is free to cast a fly to yet another fine Alaska trophy.

On another king salmon adventure, a companion and I, along with a group of other anglers, flew with Doug and Danny Brewer of Alaska West Air out of Nikiski (north Kenai) and across Cook Inlet to a small tundra lake. There, we transferred to a helicopter and lifted off for some of the most spectacular king salmon fishing I've ever experienced.

That particular afternoon provided us with something over a dozen hookups apiece. Those kings were so fresh from the ocean that they were covered with sea lice, and they were so numerous that it was almost like fishing for trout in a barrel. For weeks thereafter, however, my elbow paid a stiff price for the success we enjoyed that day. Unless you've experienced it, it's difficult to imagine the amount of strain a dozen or so powerful king salmon can cause to an angler's elbow.

Yes, I must admit, every once in a while, I still find myself dreaming about that exciting afternoon and hooking all the kings we did, most of them ranging in the 20- to 35-pound class. Actually, just flying around in that helicopter was plenty of adventure for one day. We sat back and observed as the pilot took us upstream to check out several holes. It was amazing how easily we could spot the fish from the air—even determining the numbers, sizes, and condition of the fish—and how easy it was to pick out the best hole of the bunch.

A fair percentage of the fish we encountered that day were jacks— small king salmon weighing from 5 to 12 pounds. Each of Alaska's Pacific salmon species have jacks, except for pink salmon, which are a one-year species. In a way, jacks can be viewed as being sexually mature, capricious teenagers that seemingly reenter fresh water whenever they want, frequently migrating with another species and often arriving prior to their larger counterparts. Jacks definitely assist in the spawning process; it's nature's way of adding reproductive assistance for their older brothers and helping to ensure the survival of the species.

Newcomers to king salmon fishing quickly discover that these fish can really tear an angler up, especially those anglers who insist on using light tackle. Sure, everybody wants to hook a king, but few anglers really understand what they're getting into until they do manage to hook into a fish that's ten times larger than the largest trout they've ever seen. Therefore, it shouldn't come as a surprise that king salmon ruin more fishing tackle—especially reels—than any other North American freshwater species. With a fish that can weigh 60 to 70 pounds or more attached to the end of his line, a fly fisher always gets his money's worth in a hurry—and then some.

At times, pursuing king salmon with a fly can be a frustrating experience, and it's not just battling the fish that's the problem. Often it can be difficult for a fly fisher to find suitable water that isn't either too deep or too swift or that doesn't have too many spoon-draggers and/or power-boats covering it. And when an angler does locate king water with some degree of privacy, it sometimes can be difficult to get the fly down to the fish zone. Big, deep water, which is where kings are frequently found, can make it tough on a fly fisher at times, especially on wide, deep rivers. Particularly frustrating are those times when the angler can see the shadows of kings stacked up like cordwood but can't seem to get into a position to present the fly. Yet there are those times when a fly fisher will locate kings lying in fairly accessible spots in moderately deep water and will be able to experience the true enjoyment of fly fishing for king salmon.

For those anglers who want to give kings a go with a fly rod, here is the king salmon prescription many Alaska fly fishers recommend. Combined with a pinch of luck and dash of patience, I believe this method will, sooner or later, land a fly fisher an Alaska king salmon:

1. Use a 10-weight fly rod, minimum. An 11- or 12-weight would be better still.

2. Use a high-density 20- or 24-foot sinking-tip fly line, such as a Cortland Type 6 or Teeny T-300 or T-400 series.

3. Use a 15-pound minimum, 4-foot maximum leader.

4. Use a size 2, 1/0, or 2/0 weighted fly, allowing it to get down and drift with the currents as it bounces deep along the stream bottom. A big Fat Freddy or a large, weighted Egg-Sucking Leech often performs nicely.

5. Look for seams where moderate currents join swifter water or where obstructions or structures form holding water.

6. Make many patient, quartering-upstream casts above likely looking holding water, allowing your fly to bounce for as long as possible with the currents, all the while twitching the fly slightly and keeping as much slack out of the line as possible.

7. If it feels as though you've hooked a snag, set the hook, hold on tight, and get ready for the fireworks. *Do not* attempt to muscle a behemoth king during its first powerful run, or the fish will break off. Instead, use this time to reset the hook firmly by asserting a series of firm, upward and sideward lifts. First-timers will probably want to use a barbed hook while fishing for kings, carefully releasing the fish after the battle.

8. After the fish has begun to tire out some, employ the drag on the reel, brake by attempting to palm the reel while playing the fish, or both. Attempting to muscle a large king salmon too early in the fight may result in a broken tippet, a broken reel, a snapped rod, or all three. All you want to do at this stage of the fight is tire the fish out. Usually this takes some time, frequently more than a half hour. When (and if) you finally manage to get the king to hand, you'll know you've really earned your trophy.

It's one thing to catch a large king salmon using stout spinning gear, and quite another to land such a creature on a fly rod. But one thing is for certain: Those who accomplish the task will never forget the experience.

Broadly speaking, Alaska's king salmon are found in the southern two-thirds of the state, from the saltwater regions of Ketchikan and nearby Prince of Wales Island in the southeast to Kuskokwim Bay in the west, although they can also be found around Nome, including the whole of the Seward Peninsula, and extending north along the shores of the Chukchi Sea all the way to Point Hope. Some of Alaska's most productive king salmon rivers are the Kenai, Naknek, Alagnak, Kanektok, Goodnews, Chuitna, Nushagak, Togiak, Karluk, Talachulitna, Yukon, Situk, Koktuli, Talkeetna, and Chilikadrotna, although there are many other excellent salmon fisheries as well.

The best time to fly-fish for king salmon in Alaska is from mid-June to mid-July, with the optimum time depending on the particular water and the particular salmon run. However, king salmon can be encountered in Alaska's rivers and streams throughout the summer months in varying degrees of condition, or freshness, and sometimes they are found in what might seem like outrageously small streams. Frequently, a fly fisher will

be standing in waist-deep water, fishing for another Alaska species altogether, when a huge, partially or fully spawned-out king salmon will
scurry past him, surprising him more than a little.

The timing of the various king salmon runs sometimes raises questions with fly fishers. When is the best time to schedule a trip based
around kings? If you consider June as being the *prime* month for kings,
and July as second-best, you should have no problem finding fish.

Every year, a handful of lucky anglers manage some exceptionally
large chinooks, especially Kenai kings. A few years ago, Raymond
McGuire, who owns and operates Kenai River Guide Service, managed
to boat a Kenai king, hooked on gear, that tipped the scales at 88 pounds.
And Alaska's king salmon can come larger still. The heaviest king salmon
on record was a 126-pounder, a fish that was taken commercially from
the salt waters of Prince William Sound fifty-some years ago. The tail of
that fish alone was 17½ inches wide. Today you can see this mounted
specimen at the Raspberry Office of the Alaska Department of Fish &
Game. But kings this size are the exception. The king salmon angler can
realistically expect to encounter mature fish in the 20- to 55-pound
range.

The excitement caused in Alaska by the annual arrival of king
salmon during June is something to behold. A legion of motor homes
suddenly appears from out of nowhere, a sign to Alaska residents that
summer has arrived once again. It's a short window of time in Alaska
when hotels, motels, and restaurants fairly bustle with newly arrived
fishermen of all ages, a time when airports seem barely able to handle all
of the incoming out-of-state guests.

Although Alaska's king salmon are numerous, it is important to keep
in mind that they are not an unlimited resource. With more and more
people eager to fish for king salmon each season, and with commercial
fishing pressures increasing each year, Alaska's king salmon, as well as its
king fisheries, are a fairly fragile commodity that warrant some amount
of monitoring. One of the most amazing wonders of all is how some of
Alaska's drive-to rivers can continue to support the numbers of kings
they do annually, although the numbers of kings returning to many rivers
have declined slightly over the past decade.

CHAPTER TWENTY-THREE

Silver Salmon

THE SILVER SALMON (*ONCORHYNCHUS KISUTCH*), ALSO known as the silverside, coho, autumn, or white-lipped salmon, is, broadly speaking, the Alaska fly fisher's favorite Pacific salmon species. Silver salmon, which are among the most aggressive of Alaska's salmon, are large enough to make for exciting fishing, but not *too* big, averaging 10 to 13 pounds. (The state record silver was a 26-pounder taken in 1976 at Icy Straits in southeast Alaska.) Best of all, silver salmon will attack any number of flashy fly patterns with reckless abandon.

Alaska's silvers are famed worldwide, and for good reason. They are undoubtedly Alaska's premier calling cards come August, especially for fly rodders eager to hook a good-size fish that commonly goes airborne, with striking tail-dancing and cartwheeling displays.

In early July in Alaska, with the arrival of the sockeyes, many of those who fish fairly little head out in search of an ice chest full of freshly caught salmon. Then, come late July, when the silvers arrive, both local anglers and ardent fly fishers from around the globe head out in amazing numbers for a go at silvers, the species many fly fishers consider to be the noblest of Alaska's Pacific salmon species.

The best months for fly fishing for silver salmon are August and September, with some second runs (and sometimes larger fish) returning to fresh water as late as October and November. Check with local guides or Fish & Game authorities about the best times for individual silver runs and the best places to find fish at any given time.

When a silver strikes, there's generally little or no hesitation involved; just *kazam!*—suddenly it's there at the end of your line, a 10- or 12-pound coho, flipping and cartwheeling, feeling very much like a very large rainbow gone mad. It's now an officially recognized fact that rainbow trout and Pacific salmon are more closely related than was once thought. As it turns out, silver salmon are first cousins to rainbows.

The life cycle of the silver salmon is truly amazing. Somehow, millions of tiny fry manage to survive, living off insects and minuscule pieces of decaying salmon flesh. Immature silvers spend from one to three years in fresh water before migrating, as parr, to salt water, where they'll remain and feed and grow for two or three more years before returning to fresh water to spawn at the exact spots where they were hatched. Even during the first six months of its existence, a fry has a tendency toward territoriality, particularly so in silver salmon. This trait continues on up through adulthood. Many biologists believe it's this territorial instinct that makes silvers the aggressive adversaries they are when fly fishers encounter them as they return to spawn.

As I'm a dedicated rainbow fly fisher, and silver salmon fishing occurs at about the same time as serious trophy rainbow fishing, I've rarely focused exclusively on fly fishing for silvers. I do, however, take any opportunity for silver salmon fly fishing that happens to come my way. In my travels across Alaska, I've enjoyed a lot of great fly fishing for silvers, and one of my most memorable silver experiences came entirely by accident while I was fishing for Dolly Varden char.

I fished my way very casually around a bend of one of my favorite Kenai Peninsula drive-to rivers, to be surprised by a large school of resting silvers just downstream. Since Dollies had been the only fish on my agenda that day, the only rod I'd brought along was a old, refinished Southbend bamboo dry-fly rod—a short, stiff, fairly fast-actioned 7½-footer. I hadn't been fishing dry flies that day, however; instead, I'd been nymphing tiny single-egg patterns called Pinkies, flies that are among the deadliest for attracting ravenous Dollies.

The sight of that school of dime-bright silvers finning in those currents put an immediate change in my Dolly Varden plans, and without hesitation, I decided to try for those silvers. I clipped off the single-egg pattern I'd been fishing and rigged my leader with a moderately weighted, pink, double-egg fly called a Babine Special. I was fishing a floating line with a long, tapered leader, and I replaced the tippet with 1X.

There I was, standing nearly chest-deep in a fairly secluded, small, gin-clear stream with a canopy of overhanging cottonwoods, holding a measly 7½-foot, 6-weight bamboo rod. Since the silvers were downstream from me, I climbed up the bank and managed my way through some alders to where I could circle around and approach the school of salmon from below. I carefully reentered the river some 15 yards below the salmon, trying my best not to make any sudden moves that would alert the fish.

With tall, thick brush directly behind me, my first thought was to attempt a roll cast, hoping my little bamboo rod would manage the weighted fly, but then I realized such an attempt would be fairly futile, since my fly would begin to sink before I could take up any slack and execute a presentation cast, and I would surely frighten the fish.

I finally decided my only hope was to false-cast a couple of times off to the side of the school, lengthening out enough fly line on each thrust to make an accurate presentation. I hoped the sight of my fly line whipping in the air wouldn't alarm those silvers.

Aiming and adjusting my casting timing as carefully as I could, I plunked my two-egg fly into a confluence above a small seam that appeared to flow directly by the school. Nothing much happened on the first drift, although a couple of silvers nudged closer to the pack at the sight of my passing fly. I picked up and cast again, attempting to land the fly slightly closer to the fish.

When I did, one of the silvers near the head of the pack peeled off and suddenly lunged at my fly. I'd hooked one!

Now the only questions were: (a) Would my tippet hold? and (b) Could my little cane rod manage a 10- or 12-pound silver salmon? Quite frankly, I had no idea; all I knew was that somehow, suddenly, I had a silver salmon attached to the end of my line and my tiny rod now felt like a mere toy.

The reel I was fishing that day was a little Hardy Marquis #5, and I was just starting to worry whether it was big enough to handle the task, when I realized the coho had circled and was headed directly for me. It was a rather tight little setting there, fairly deep with a moderate flow but without much distance between banks. So I took in slack.

Suddenly the coho came powering out of the water, splashing me with a showering spray, then dived and dashed back to the school again for security. I attempted to maintain my balance and hold onto that little fly rod for dear life. Eventually, after several more showery cartwheels and half gainers, the coho began to tire out some. All the while, I carefully worked in fly line, finally managing the fish over to where I could reach out and eventually tail it, revive it, and remove the hook. As I released the fish, I smiled as I watched it scurry directly back to the school.

Since I hadn't heard any sounds of splintering bamboo and my rod did not appear to have been harmed, and since the school was still finning there in the currents, I decided to give it another go.

My second hookup didn't come for about another four or five casts, but it finally did come, the next fish seeming to strike out of sheer irritation at the sight of my fly. Almost before I knew it, my little Hardy reel was a blur again, only this time I made sure I pointed my rod directly at my quarry to ensure that the fish's power wouldn't break the rod tip, although this placed additional pressure on the tippet.

Amazingly, after releasing the second, I was able to coax a third silver to the fly before the school had finally had enough and began finning upstream around the bend. The action had been fast and furious. It had probably lasted only about a half hour or so, but for me it had been an afternoon of silver salmon fly fishing at its finest, even though it took place just 100 yards off the main highway.

One can't be a fairly active fly fisher and live in Alaska for very long without compiling a rather decent history of great experiences with silver salmon. Another of my most memorable days of fishing cohos occurred on the Kamishak River, about 5 miles upstream from where the river's clear waters empty into Kamishak Bay, on the west side of Cook Inlet across from Homer and Seldovia.

The wonderful but wild Kami is not far from Alaska's famed McNeil River, where several large brown bears frequent the area. We must have sighted more than a dozen that day, but since the presence of bears often means good numbers of fish, my two companions and I viewed the bears as a good omen.

The coho fishing we experienced that day in late August was spectacular. Our guides looked for slack-water areas alongside the river— places where traveling salmon frequently pull over to rest. If you locate one of these temporary sanctuaries, you should definitely pursue it. Use a size 2 Flash Fly or a large Egg-Sucking Leech or something similar and a fairly high-density sinking-tip line, letting the fly sink a bit before beginning a medium-fast strip retrieve. Be ready for a strike. Silvers are aggressive and don't take kindly to uninvited intruders. Even when resting from their laborious upstream journeys, silvers are territorial and make for immediate adversaries.

For three straight hours, the three of us battled those powerful salmon until our arms ached. Large brown bears wandered around us the entire day. Our guides took turns wading out into the main channel to talk to a bear whenever one would turn up, keeping it away while the rest of us battled cohos. We averaged some twenty fish apiece that day.

One of the beauties of Alaska's various runs of silver salmon is that they are very widespread. The best silver salmon fishing generally occurs in coastal rivers fairly near the salt, although some runs can be found far inland. Like the kings, silver salmon are found mostly in the southern two-thirds of Alaska, although good silver runs surround much of the state, from Point Hope to the north of Kotzebue, the whole of the Alaska Peninsula (where silvers over 20 pounds are routinely taken), and south to Ketchikan. Great Alaska silver flows include the Kenai, Chuitna, Talachulitna, Silver Salmon Creek, Kamishak, Togiak, Alagnak, Karluk, Ugashik, Goodnews, Kanektok, Situk, Thorne, and a smattering of unnamed streams on the Alaska Peninsula where the silvers are huge.

Saltwater estuaries are frequently prime spots for locating silvers. Look for slack-water resting areas along riversides where schools of cohos pull over to rest during their upstream migrations. Also look for seams where faster water converges with moderate water, because silver salmon (like steelhead) like to lie up in these spots and clear their gills before continuing upstream. Watch for silvers stacking up at riffles, highly aerated zones where salmon will often stop to take in oxygen and revive themselves before continuing their upstream journeys. Fairly deep riffles are excellent places for locating holding fish, and like all fish species, silver salmon seem to feel protected when they hold under a broken surface.

Flash Flies, Egg-Sucking Leeches, and large purple, silver, and orange Fall Favorites are effective on silvers, and black and brown Woolly Buggers perform admirably also. A stout 8- or 9-weight rod is about right for battling fresh, dime-bright silvers, and 1X (12-pound) is about the minimum strength I'd suggest for tippet material.

Silvers can also be taken at the surface, a practice often touted by those who've experienced it. Pink and chartreuse deer-hair creations (looking something like a half-completed mouse pattern or, better yet, a deer-hair version of a hammerhead shark) called Wogs (short for Polly Wogs) will frequently tempt feisty silvers to strike at the surface. All of a sudden, a big mouth appears above the surface and engulfs the highly visible fly, and the game is on!

One of the latest crazes is float tubing for silvers. I haven't tried it, but I know two fly fishers who make one or two pilgrimages to Kodiak Island each fall to float-fish for powerhouse silver salmon just in from the salt. There's a small lake just upstream from salt water, easily reachable from the road, that makes a great place for float tubers to hook cohos and get dragged around for an hour or so in the process.

Silver salmon are not a limitless commodity, so whenever possible, practice catch and release. Take just enough fish for the freezer, and allow any extras to complete their spawning. Silvers make for fine dining, although red and king salmon are considered superior in taste.

CHAPTER TWENTY-FOUR

Chums

As far as many experienced fly fishers are concerned, Alaska's prize for the most underrated salmon must go to the chum *(Oncorhynchus keta),* Alaska's most widespread salmon species.

Truth is, the chum, also called the calico, dog salmon, or silverbrite, can rip a spool free of backing as fast as any fish in Alaska. Hook a bright chum a couple of miles above salt water, and you'll quickly learn that these fish are no pushovers. They often supply fly fishers with some exciting topwater action, frequently doing half gainers and complete back flips, not to mention powering away with impressive rooster tails in their wake. Alaska's chum salmon are fish in the 8- to 20-pound bracket.

Bobby DeVito, owner of Branch River Lodge on the Alagnak, introduced me to the chum, now one of my favorite Alaska species, and also to one of my favorite chum flies: a size 2, pink-and-purple Popsicle. I've also experienced superb fly fishing for chums with silvery Flash Flies (particularly when fishing slightly deeper water) and purple Egg-Sucking Leeches. In less-than-knee-deep currents, chums seem particularly attracted to large purple and hot pink flies, as well as orange creations, whether the flies are fished intermediate style (6 to 12 inches under the surface), at a stream bottom, or skated along the surface, depending upon the current speed and water depth.

Generally speaking, one of the foremost secrets of successfully fishing Pacific salmon is to get the fly down to where the fish are. Newcomers often waste countless hours drifting and stripping flies over the heads of salmon when they should be employing a high-density sinking-tip line and a 3½-foot leader. Try stripping a silvery Flash Fly, or a big, ugly

146

Egg-Sucking Leech, or perhaps a pink-and-purple Popsicle or Show Girl pattern through a school of milling silverbrites with such a rig and be ready for action!

Chums also have the wonderful habit of chasing surface patterns, and flies such as a pink, deer-hair Wog can prove to be extremely effective and a joy to fish. The correct technique is to employ a floating line and allow a big, intentional downstream loop to form at the surface, causing a floating fly to skate across the surface. Recently, more radical patterns—floaters such as the newly devised MicroWog (a smaller version of a pink deer-hair dry) and large, hot-pink- or cerise-tied standard drys such as pink Humpy patterns—have also proven effective in the taking of chums at the surface.

Most fly fishers are astounded at the power of their first chum salmon. Truth is, when ol' calico takes a fly and decides to move to the next county, you'd better be ready to begin reel control. Pound for pound, the chum just might walk away with the all-Alaska power-to-weight honors. It's no wonder a growing number of fly fishers are visiting Alaska in mid- to late July with chums in mind. A Bristol Bay lodge owner recently told me that some 25 percent of his clients schedule visits to his lodge during July especially to experience the thrill of Alaska's annual chum run.

Suggested fly rods for chum salmon are 9- and 10-weights. That might sound like a lot of rod, but that's what you'll need for these powerful fish. I'd choose 10-weight over a 9-weight, especially for chums near the salt, where they frequently seem to develop an additional 50 horsepower.

Opinions differ regarding appropriate fly reels for chum salmon. Some anglers feel that a reel with a stout drag is a necessity on a fish so powerful; others believe that click reels (trout reels) are sufficient, as they add an element of thrill and surprise to the fishing. Beginners might want to start with drag-equipped reels, but ultimately, you should select the reel you feel most comfortable with.

To hook chums, I recommend looking for congregating, milling schools, especially in wide, knee-deep-or-less, moderately moving water. Chums prefer low-gradient rivers, ones that don't rise steeply out of salt water. In swift-moving water, try tumbling a pink-and-purple creation, such as a Popsicle or a Show Girl, along the bottom to resting fish. In swifter currents, chums seem to be highly attracted to bright, flashy patterns, and a Flash Fly often works wonders. Use a fairly high-density sinking-tip line to get your fly down quickly to where the salmon are holding or milling about. Employ stout 1X (12-pound) mono at a minimum, or better yet, use 0X leaders. Allow the fly to swing through suspected holding areas, keeping as much slack out of the fly line as possible.

Chum salmon commonly arrive around the third week of July. The best time for fly fishing for chums is late July through early August. Chums are found throughout most of Alaska, averaging 9 to 12 pounds and commonly weigh up to 15 or even 18 pounds. The Alaska record chum, taken in 1985, registered an amazing 32 pounds.

Chum salmon is not generally considered one of the best tasting of Alaska's Pacific salmon, although those who eat them say chums are definitely best when fresh or if they're dried or smoked.

Be that as it may, there's simply no better fish in Alaska than a power-house calico to prepare you for a go at a king salmon on a fly.

CHAPTER TWENTY-FIVE

Sockeye Salmon

 ONE OF MY FAVORITE ALASKA SPORT FISH IS THE SOCKEYE, or red, salmon *(Oncorhynchus nerka)*. This fish is a plankton eater and therefore has no business, whatsoever, striking at artificials. But then, technically, sockeyes don't really *strike* at flies; rather, they tend to nip at them. And that's when all the fun begins.

Although I tend to be geared toward rainbow fishing above all else, I enjoy having a go at a sockeye every now and then. Pound for pound, the sockeye just might be the strongest fighter of Alaska's Pacific salmon species, except for possibly the chum salmon.

Some years ago, on a bend of the Kenai River near the Great Alaska Fish Camp, I hooked a spectacular fresh, mint-bright, super-strong "blueback," a sockeye salmon that had just arrived from the salt—my first blueback on a fly rod.

Camp manager Lawrence John and guide Mike Murri had no sooner suggested that I try casting a T-300 sinking-tip line to a certain confluence, when *wham!*—a 9-pound blueback hit my fly and immediately turned sideways in the Kenai's powerful currents. Before I knew it, that sockeye had about 90 yards of my backing out and was still very much in the process of taking backing as it sped downstream at an alarming pace. I was amazed at the speed of my whirling reel, surprised that the spool wasn't freewheeling and thus creating a bird's nest of loose, tangled backing at my feet. Before that day, I hadn't been aware that any salmon other than the chinook could apply that kind of power.

Sockeyes have a way of testing even the most experienced angler's skills, it seems, especially when they're hooked in swift currents. Upon feeling the metal, sockeyes frequently peel off and head directly for fast water, allowing the currents to assist them in their getaway attempts. A sockeye's fight is tenacious indeed, and each year, tens of thousands of residents and visitors alike flock to Alaska's salmon rivers to have a go at hooking a few of these "skyrocketing sockeyes." It doesn't hurt matters much that the red salmon is considered one of the best tasting of Alaska's salmon species.

After sockeyes have been in fresh water for a few days, they, more than other Pacific salmon, begin a very dramatic color change. The sockeye's body begins to turn a deep red, and its head turns a parrot green. At the same time, the lower jaw develops an extremely hooked kype.

There is a marked difference in the way a spawning sockeye applies power to a battle compared with how a blueback fights. For a few weeks before and at the time of spawning, sockeyes are much easier to hook than when they first enter fresh water. Sockeyes fiercely guard their redds, or nests, so once they've begun spawning, they will often snap at just about any object that appears to be invading their temporary spawning domain—including a fly. Although sockeyes caught under these conditions can still provide an angler with a good, enjoyable battle, it's not nearly the challenge of those that are just entering fresh water. To my mind, bluebacks are really the only sockeyes worth bragging about.

Here are some of the secrets I've learned about hooking and landing mint-bright sockeyes successfully on a fly. The best fishing for bluebacks is often found in moderate to swift-moving waters. If you come upon a school of sockeyes milling about in slow water, the fish often are too easily snagged or foul-hooked on fins or flanks, and there is seldom much sport to be found. To get fresh sockeyes to take a fly, look for swifter water, such as deep riffles, or possibly a moderately deep confluence where a main river and a tributary meet. You're likely to find resting salmon at these places, holding right along the bottom, attempting to regain their strength and cleaning out their gills, which often pick up silt on their upstream migration.

Use a high-density sinking-tip line if the water you're fishing has any depth to it. In shallower waters, you can get away with fishing a floating line and using a split shot or two or lead twist-ons to help get the fly down. Remember, getting *down* to Pacific salmon in fresh water is extremely important. Otherwise, you can waste many hours drifting flies over hundreds of salmon without experiencing success. Employ a fairly small but large-gaped, sparsely tied, brown, purple, or pink shrimp pattern. (Mike Hershberger relied on his own dark creation, which he called Fred the Red, similar to a Teeny Nymph, tied with pheasant tail.)

Casting upstream, quartering across the currents, employing a high-density, sinking-tip line, you would do well to position your fly so that it gets down quickly, and allow the fly to drift with the currents directly into any suspected lie. Bouncing a fly along a river's bottom, minimizing any slack in the fly line, will likely maximize your chances of enticing sockeyes to nip.

Two of my favorite places for finding fresh, incoming bluebacks are the Kenai River, just at its confluence with the Moose, near Sterling; and the Newhalen River, just below the rapids where the deeper, swifter currents form a seam with the shallow currents, about a half mile upstream from where the river flows into Iliamna Lake. There are hundreds of other exceptional, easily accessible spots for bluebacks. One of the most famed and easily accessed is the ever-popular Russian River, just upstream from its confluence with the Kenai. The Kvichak River (the outlet of Iliamna Lake) can be superb sockeye water, providing both deep-water and braided-water opportunities at the largest sockeye salmon run in the world.

Sockeyes typically weigh from 6 to 9 pounds, with some larger specimens tipping the scales at 10 to 12 pounds. The Alaska record sockeye, taken at the Kenai River in 1974, weighed 16 pounds.

July 4 usually marks the beginning of really good sockeye salmon fishing throughout Alaska, and early July is the time for encountering numbers of bluebacks.

Although it's fashionable for some fly anglers to fish 7-weight fly rods for sockeyes, Alaska's best sockeye outfits are unquestionably the 8- and 9-weights. Yes, you could probably land a sockeye salmon using a 3-weight fly rod, but that doesn't make it the proper tool for the job. I still rely on an old, battle-scarred 9-weight graphite rod that has proven to be very lucky for me over the years. I find the Teeny (or similar) sinking-tip fly lines best for fishing to sockeyes in moderate-depth water, with the 200-grain line being my general favorite, depending upon the water depths.

First-timers might want to use reels with modern drag systems, but fly fishing for sockeyes with conventional nondrag reels can make for great sport if you have adequate backing on your reel. In the end, it boils down to the amount of time you want to devote to playing each fish. If you can enjoy a battle for a while, conventional reels usually prove to be adequate.

One thing's for certain: If you can master the subtle techniques of hooking fresh sockeyes, these bluebacks will definitely earn your respect.

CHAPTER TWENTY-SIX

Pink Salmon

 THE PINK SALMON (*ONCORHYNCHUS GORBUSCHA*) DEFInitely is not a pretty fish. With its long, ghoulish snout and its outlandish, sharply humped back, a returning male "humpy" can look downright startling, even disgusting at times, even though, when just taken from salt water, pinks can appear astoundingly brilliant.

But pink salmon do have the wonderful habit of gobbling flies of nearly every shape, color, and kind every chance they get, and because of this, pink salmon can make for extremely great fun on a fly rod. In fact, if someone was to ask me what would be the best species for teaching someone how to fly-fish Alaska, my response unquestionably would be the pink salmon.

Sometimes, when guests appear from the Lower 48 and ask to go out fishing, I'll refer them to Resurrection Creek, near the town of Hope, across Turnagain Arm from Anchorage, a place I call the Pink Salmon Capital of the World. This is far from being accurate, of course, because there are hundreds of similar intertidal areas close to salt water surrounding Alaska in which fly fishers can discover pinks, but then, Hope is only an hour and a half from Anchorage, and during mid- and late July, especially in even years, it generally provides excellent pink salmon fishing. In even years, much more than odd, when pinks arrive in force, they frequently are so thick in the water that it's fairly difficult to find a place to wade out among the fish to make a cast. With its easy access and its battalions of eager pink salmon, Hope makes a superb spot for a beginner to learn the basics of salmon fishing.

Pinks are found at most intertidal areas surrounding Alaska, from salt water inland for approximately 15 miles or thereabouts, so if you're hunting for pink salmon in numbers, you should fish very near the salt.

The best times to fish for Alaska's pink salmon are from mid-July to mid-August. Pinks are the most prolific of Alaska's salmon species, especially during even years, when they enter the state's intertidal areas by the hundreds of thousands to spawn and quickly die. All of a sudden they're just there—pinks by the thousands—and many a stream mouth along Alaska's coast becomes swollen with them. Pinks do not remain prime, or fresh, for any length of time once they've entered fresh water to spawn, but deteriorate surprisingly quickly.

Pinks spend only one year at sea before returning to fresh water, which they do only every other year. All other species of Pacific salmon have good numbers of fish that find their way to fresh water to spawn annually. Not so with pinks. Although there is a small percentage of odd-year pink arrivals, pinks always reenter freshwater in droves during even years.

When you stand and look into a current and try to spot pinks, frequently the first thing you'll see is the black-and-white outline of a single fish finning in a clear, shallow riffle. Then, typically, a moment later you'll observe yet another fish, and then another, and still another, until you realize there are maybe even fifty or a hundred humpies—everywhere!

Pink salmon are easily the smallest of Alaska's salmon species, averaging only 3 to 5 pounds, but many of the bigger males far outweigh that mark, often going 7 or 8 pounds. The Alaska record pink salmon, taken near Sterling in 1974, near where the Moose River enters the Kenai, weighed 12 pounds, 9 ounces.

CHAPTER TWENTY-SEVEN

Northern Pike

"THE NORTHERN PIKE IS THE 'DRAGSTER' OF THE FISH family" is how I overheard one young Alaska fishing guide describe *Esox lucius* to a client, and I must admit, somehow this description seems to fit the northern pike very well, indeed. These cagey, multitoothed, sinister-looking, torpedo-shaped, yellow-bellied, yellow-and-green-camouflaged wolves of the tundra swamps lie hidden in their weedy domains until something edible-looking swims along, manages to get their attention, and suddenly triggers a pike's vicious strike mechanism.

When a northern pike switches on its afterburners, it's fully committed, and like a sidewinder missile (and very much like a barracuda), Mr. Pike is suddenly on track, straight to his target, until he either sinks his hundreds of razor-sharp teeth into his victim and drags it down to a watery grave, or misses and slinks back to his murky bed. It is said that ducklings and goslings are in grave danger while swimming near pike habitat, which I have no reason to doubt.

A pike's principal food source is other fish, including other pike, as well as myriad salmon parr and trout fry, but they also thrive on crayfish and frogs and, in warmer climates, snakes. Actually, the question is, what *won't* a pike eat? In fact, just this past season, after a day's rainbow fishing, one of the guides showed us a 16-inch rainbow trout that he'd discovered entombed in the belly of a 24-inch pike a client had taken.

Alaska is loaded with excellent pike-fishing waters. The most talked-about pike country in Alaska is the Minto Flats region in the middle of the state, slightly west of Fairbanks, but don't rule out discovering pike at many of Alaska's thousands of other slack-water areas, including several

154

very productive areas near the Canadian border. In fact, good northern pike fishing can be found in over 80 percent of the state, the Pacific rim of the Alaska Peninsula and south-central Alaska's Kenai Peninsula excepted. All of those myriad unnamed tundra lakes dotting Alaska's interior flatlands are very likely spots for discovering northerns, provided there is some amount of constant flow present to aerate the water. In Alaska, if a place looks like it should harbor pike, chances are fairly good that it does.

Although pike are pure, unadulterated adrenaline on a fly rod and can be exceptionally enjoyable to hook, I don't know many fly anglers who take pike fishing too seriously, especially with all the other fish species Alaska offers. Nevertheless, pike fishing does make for great sport every now and then, and its popularity is definitely on the increase.

To hook a northern pike every now and then, a fly fisher doesn't need to undertake a trip fashioned specifically around pike. Salmon and char rivers often have stillwater offshoots or little-visited side waters—areas that contain pike, and sometimes very large specimens, indeed.

For a break in the action from the regular fishing in the main currents, try venturing along one or two of the many offshoots rivers frequently feature, and then try tossing a large, colorful, gaudy-looking streamer—something like a big, tattered, red-and-white Lefty's Deceiver or a Sea-Habit, perhaps, or a Dahlberg Diver surface pattern—over near the weeds and water lilies in these slower-water estuaries, where pike are likely lying in wait for one form or another of food to happen by. After slapping the water with your presentation, retrieve the fly by stripping back with quick, jerky movements, or for ever better results, employ a sinking-tip line. (I used to think pike fishing was best at the surface, but I've found I have a much higher percentage of hookups with sinking-tip lines.)

Pike are not selective feeders. What they do strike at most often, it seems, is something big and hairy, something appearing fairly alive, frequently something bordering on a saltwater pattern. For surface fishing, nothing seems to work better than a big, hairy mouse imitation, so get ready for quick action when retrieving one of these deadly, floating patterns. Actually, the pattern doesn't even have to look much like a mouse. Got an old candy bar wrapper? Wad it up around a large hook, toss it over near the weeds or lilies, begin your retrieve, and hold on securely. If you're anywhere near good pike water, before you know it, you'll probably see the rush of a big, toothy northern.

Success with pike, I've found, usually happens quickly or it doesn't happen at all. Sometimes a second cast is needed, however—employing slower strips, perhaps—to trigger a fish that might have been caught napping when the first "meal" slipped by.

Although the initial strike of a northern is sudden, and the fish is frequently depicted as being a tenacious fighter, northern pike are not renowned for prolonged battles. Smaller pike, frequently referred to as "hammer handles," are numerous in many of Alaska's off-the-beaten-path waters and offer great fun, especially when fished on one of the lighter-weight fly rods. Beginners will probably want to wear gloves and use pliers when removing hooks from a pike's mouth, for a pike's numerous teeth are razor-sharp. As with barracuda, holding a pike upside down while removing a hook is a good way of temporarily subduing its predatory instincts.

In south-central Alaska, Hewitt Lake, near Skwentna, is usually good pike water, as are the series of lakes just above the Yentna River, very near where Lake Creek enters in.

A few years ago, a friend revealed his favorite method of hooking northern pike. One day, he said, while he was hurrying to motor across a small, pike-filled lake in a small boat, he inadvertently allowed a colorful, long-shanked streamer to drag along in the wake. Suddenly he saw his rod lurch. He lunged to grab it, and sure enough, a very large fish had struck his streamer pattern and was well hooked. He killed the outboard motor and turned to battling the fish. It wasn't until he got the fish near the boat that he realized he'd hooked a pike. He didn't have a scale, but he estimated it to be around 18 or 20 pounds. The minute he lifted the fish, he knew he was hooked on fly fishing for northern pike.

"Where *is* this lake?" I asked him, trying to sound matter-of-fact. He only smiled, although he later told me the general area.

On another trip, he deliberately repeated the same tactics, experiencing similar results, and decided this was great sport. He began to realize that hookups only improved the faster he cranked his little 3-horsepower motor. Soon, whether the trout fishing at a nearby river was good that day or not, my friend found himself trolling for pike quite regularly. Granted, my friend's method was far from being "classic" Alaska fly fishing, although it was similar to a successful method for fishing barracuda in the Caribbean.

A few years back, while on a salmon and char trip, my dad and I inadvertently discovered superb northern pike fishing at several of the stillwater offshoots and sloughs we explored along the Fish River, near White Mountain, some 80 miles east of Nome. It didn't take us long to realize what great fun it was to slip silently along many of those seldom frequented offshoots in a johnboat, venturing back into those remote channels that very few people explore. Good pike water is usually slow moving and gin clear, often a free-running, chest-high current, as pike require aerated water.

Several pike "experts" like to expound on how necessary wire leaders are for taking northerns, but it's been my experience that common, everyday, 25-pound monofilament will usually handle a few small to medium-size northerns before it becomes necessary to change the leader. I don't know about large pike, however, since the largest northern I've ever managed on a fly was just over 33 inches.

Fishing for northern pike in Alaska is at its best during the warm summer months of June, July, and August, and the highest concentrations of pike are generally to be found in the northern two-thirds of the state. The official Alaska record for northern pike was a 38-pounder taken in 1978 at a spot called Fish Creek. (I've found twenty-seven places called Fish Creek on my Alaska map, although I'm willing to bet this particular Fish Creek is one fairly near the Canadian border.)

Talk is sometimes heard about waters containing northerns weighing over 40 pounds, but so far no one has caught one, at least not officially. Actually, the last 30-pound pike I got a fairly close glimpse of looked so fierce that I wouldn't even want to find myself in the same water as a real live, honest-to-goodness 40-pounder. A native fishing guide who lives in a small community outside Nome once told me that as a boy, he and his friends frequently would borrow their fathers' rifles and hunt northerns the size of fire logs. From time to time over the years, I've heard reports of 50-pound northerns, but in reality, any pike 30 pounds or more is a real trophy.

CHAPTER TWENTY-EIGHT

Sheefish

A DISCUSSION OF SPORTFISH SPECIES IN THE GREAT LAND would be incomplete without briefly mentioning one of the least-known and least-fished-for species in all of Alaska and North America. Fly fishers who wish to experience the truly exotic during their fishing vacations should consider making a trip to northwestern Alaska to pursue this elusive relative of the arctic grayling and common whitefish: the large-scaled, silvery-sided sheefish *(Stenodus leucichthys)*. Found—when they can be found—in the most inaccessible, remote regions of Alaska, sheefish are so rarely caught that they earned the name "inconnu" (unknown) from early French explorers.

Finding and landing inconnu is admittedly a challenge, but it can be an ultimate wilderness fly-fishing experience. Fortunately, there are a few fishing lodges and charter operations today that specialize in transporting adventurous fly fishers to the backcountry realm of the sheefish. There are two key conditions for a successful sheefishing expedition: The weather must cooperate, allowing access to sheefish waters; and fly fishers who operate on their own, without the help of knowledgeable guides, must rely on luck to find the migratory sheefish, especially during their fall spawning journeys. Fortunately, when sheefish are found, they are likely to be found in good numbers.

Sheefish exist primarily in the north-central and northwestern parts of the state, primarily in the Selawik, Kobuk, Kuskokwim, and Yukon drainages. The Kobuk River is easily the most talked-about sheefish water, and it holds the largest sheefish, but the tributaries of the massive and silty Yukon—downstream, near the river's mouth—hold the greatest numbers of sheefish of any Alaska drainage. In the Kuskokwim, too, sheefish are primarily found downstream, nearer tidal water. Lesser numbers of sheefish are known to exist in sections of the Koyukuk River, at least as far north and east as the village of Alatna, while some sheefish swim in rivers just north of Fairbanks. Guides and lodges based in the Kotzebue, Noorvike, Selawik, and Aniak areas are excellent starting points for fly fishers determined to pursue the elusive sheefish.

The general shape of the silvery sheefish, with its large mouth and protruding lower jaw, explains its nickname, "tarpon of the North." Like Florida snook, which they also resemble, sheefish typically weigh between 5 and 18 pounds. Thirty- and 35-pound sheefish are also taken fairly regularly in Alaska, and the all-time state record was an astounding 53-pound whopper landed in 1986 at the Pah River.

Sheefish typically lie deep in deep water. Anglers who successfully locate, hook, and land sheefish usually accomplish the feat using stout 12- and 15-pound spinning gear cast into deep, moderate-flowing rivers, and retrieved deep along a graveled stream bottom. Fly fishers must present their flies deeply and get them down quickly in front of the holding fish, an approach best achieved by casting a high-density sinking-tip fly line or a floating line with a weighted, extra-long leader, depending on water depth. Large, flashy smelt, leech, or streamer patterns are likely to provide the best results.

Initially, hooking a sheefish is like hooking into a large, heavy sunken log. It is during the last stages of a fight with a sheefish that the fly fisher begins to experience the powerful surges of the fish—its sudden thrashing, twisting, and cartwheeling. Larger, adult sheefish are both dwellers and fighters in the deep; they prefer to stay low until the last moments of the fight. On the other hand, smaller sheefish—5 pounds and under—are more likely to go airborne earlier in the struggle.

The best time for sheefishing is in early and midsummer, when the water warms up a bit and the most energetic fights occur. June and July are ideal months for stalking and landing this wily fish. In late September and early October, sheefish quit feeding altogether and concentrate on swimming to their upstream spawning grounds. After spawning, adult sheefish return quickly to their familiar saltwater haunts and begin feeding again. Sheefish generally overwinter near saltwater estuaries until the ice breaks up in spring.

One of the most appealing aspects of an Alaska sheefishing trip is the vast remoteness of typical sheefish country, most of which is rugged and largely treeless. These wild, beautiful regions offer panoramic views of untouched wilderness. Temperate summer nights, illuminated by the midnight sun, invite anglers to fish nearly around the clock if they wish. In sheefish territory, fly fishers can find utter solitude; the crowds simply are not there. A couple of buddies can sit back and relax in their camp after a long day's fishing and not be bothered by the distractions of life in the city, with nothing but the cool breezes and perhaps the smell of dinner sizzling over an open fire to occupy their thoughts.

While mounting a successful sheefishing excursion requires a bit of luck with the weather and good timing with fish migration, chances are good that individuals who experience Alaska sheefishing will become backcountry aficionados. They will have learned what wilderness fly fishing in the Great Land is all about.

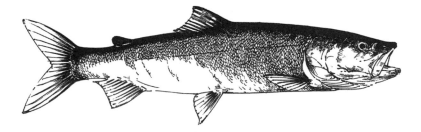

Alaska's Premier Rivers, Lakes & Streams

 OVER THE YEARS, VARIOUS LISTS HAVE BEEN COMPILED detailing Alaska's premier rivers and fisheries and the fish species found there. Here is my list, based on what I've experienced firsthand, as well as what I have gleaned from others. It should be noted that a few of Alaska's smaller premier fisheries have been purposely omitted, mainly because some are simply too small and too fragile to withstand an onslaught of fishing pressure.

RIVERS, LAKES & STREAMS	Rainbow Trout	Steelhead	King Salmon	Chum Salmon	Sockeye Salmon	Silver Salmon	Pink Salmon	Dolly Varden & Arctic Char	Lake Trout	Arctic Grayling	Sheefish	Northern Pike	Cutthroat Trout
Agulowak River	✓		✓	✓	✓	✓	✓	✓		✓			
Agulukpak River	✓				✓			✓		✓			
Alagnak River or Branch	✓		✓	✓	✓	✓	✓	✓	✓	✓		✓	
Aleknagik Lake	✓		✓	✓	✓	✓	✓	✓		✓		✓	
Alexander Creek	✓		✓	✓	✓	✓	✓	✓		✓			
American Creek	✓				✓			✓					
Anchor River	✓	✓	✓			✓	✓	✓					
Aniak River	✓		✓	✓		✓	✓	✓		✓			
Brooks River	✓				✓	✓		✓	✓	✓			
Buskin River (Kodiak)						✓	✓	✓					
Chatanika River							✓	✓		✓			
Chilikadrotna River	✓		✓	✓	✓	✓	✓	✓		✓			
Chuitna (or Chuit) River	✓		✓			✓	✓	✓					
Clear Creek	✓		✓			✓	✓			✓			
Copper River	✓				✓			✓		✓			
Council River				✓		✓	✓	✓		✓		✓	
Crescent Lake	✓							✓		✓			
Deep Creek	✓	✓	✓			✓	✓	✓					
Dream Creek	✓				✓			✓		✓			
Fish River			✓	✓		✓	✓	✓		✓		✓	
Frazer River (Kodiak)		✓				✓	✓	✓					
Gibraltar River	✓				✓			✓					
Goodnews River	✓		✓	✓	✓	✓	✓	✓		✓			
Gulkana River	✓	✓	✓			✓	✓	✓					
Holitna River			✓	✓		✓	✓	✓		✓	✓		
Iliamna River	✓				✓			✓					
Kakhonak River	✓				✓			✓		✓			
Kamishak River			✓	✓		✓	✓	✓		✓			
Kanektok River	✓		✓	✓	✓	✓	✓	✓		✓			
Karluk River (Kodiak)		✓	✓			✓	✓	✓					
Karta River (Prince of Wales Island)		✓			✓	✓	✓	✓					✓
Kenai Lake (Outlet)	✓		✓		✓	✓	✓	✓					
Kenai River	✓		✓		✓	✓	✓	✓					
Kisaralik River	✓		✓	✓		✓	✓	✓		✓			

RIVERS, LAKES & STREAMS	Rainbow Trout	Steelhead	King Salmon	Chum Salmon	Sockeye Salmon	Silver Salmon	Pink Salmon	Dolly Varden & Arctic Char	Lake Trout	Arctic Grayling	Sheefish	Northern Pike	Cutthroat Trout
Klawock River ★	✓	✓				✓							
Kobuk River				✓				✓		✓	✓	✓	
Koktuli River	✓		✓	✓	✓	✓	✓	✓		✓			
Koyuk River			✓	✓		✓	✓	✓		✓			
Kukaklek Lake	✓			✓	✓	✓	✓	✓	✓	✓			
Kulik River	✓				✓	✓		✓	✓	✓			
Kvichak River	✓		✓	✓	✓	✓	✓	✓	✓	✓		✓	
Lake Creek	✓		✓	✓	✓	✓	✓	✓		✓			
Lake Louise									✓	✓			
Lewis Creek	✓		✓	✓		✓	✓	✓					
Little Willow			✓		✓		✓			✓			
Minto Flats										✓		✓	
Mulchatna River	✓		✓	✓	✓	✓	✓	✓		✓			
Naknek Lake	✓		✓		✓	✓	✓		✓	✓		✓	
Naknek River	✓		✓	✓	✓	✓	✓	✓	✓	✓			
Nerka Lake	✓				✓	✓		✓	✓	✓		✓	
Newhalen River	✓				✓			✓	✓	✓			
Ninilchik River	✓	✓	✓			✓	✓	✓					
Noatak River				✓	✓	✓	✓	✓		✓		✓	
Nome River						✓	✓			✓			
Nonvianuk Lake	✓			✓	✓	✓	✓	✓	✓	✓			
North River			✓	✓		✓	✓	✓		✓			
Nushagak River	✓		✓	✓	✓	✓	✓	✓		✓		✓	
Nuyakuk Lake	✓				✓			✓		✓			
Nuyakuk River	✓				✓			✓		✓			
Russian River	✓		✓		✓			✓					
Selawik River				✓				✓			✓	✓	
Sheep Creek	✓		✓			✓	✓	✓					
Situk River		✓	✓			✓		✓					
Skilak Lake	✓		✓		✓	✓	✓	✓	✓				
Swanson River System	✓							✓					
Talachulitna River	✓		✓	✓	✓	✓	✓	✓		✓			
Talarik Creek (Lower)	✓				✓			✓					
Talkeetna River	✓		✓	✓		✓	✓	✓		✓			
Tazimina River	✓				✓					✓			
Theodore	✓		✓			✓	✓	✓		✓			

★ *also, salt species*

RIVERS, LAKES & STREAMS	FISH SPECIES												
	Rainbow Trout	Steelhead	King Salmon	Chum Salmon	Sockeye Salmon	Silver Salmon	Pink Salmon	Dolly Varden & Arctic Char	Lake Trout	Arctic Grayling	Sheefish	Northern Pike	Cutthroat Trout
Thorne River (Prince of Wales Island)		✓		✓		✓	✓	✓					✓
Tikchik Lake	✓							✓	✓	✓			
Togiak River	✓		✓	✓	✓	✓	✓	✓		✓		✓	
Uganik River (Kodiak)		✓	✓		✓	✓	✓	✓					
Ugashik Lakes					✓	✓		✓		✓			
Unalakleet River			✓	✓		✓	✓	✓		✓			
Willow River	✓		✓			✓	✓	✓					
Wulik River				✓				✓		✓			

ABOUT THE AUTHOR

For over a decade now, Dan Heiner has pursued his dream of fly-fishing Alaska's premier rivers, lakes, and streams. Beginning as field editor and then later serving as managing editor for *Alaska Outdoors* magazine, Dan has traveled throughout the remote regions of a state one-fifth the size of the Lower 48 combined. Always looking to add yet another Alaska river to his list, Dan has fished a good number of the state's eighty-five premier waters. All the while, Dan's appreciation for Alaska, its peoples, its rivers, and its fish has continued to grow.

Dan and his wife, Anne, have lived in Anchorage since 1983. He is currently a member of the G. Loomis, Inc., Alaska Prostaff. Dan's articles have appeared in *Flyfishing, Salmon Trout Steelhead, Safari, Alaska Outdoors,* and *Alaska Outdoor Times.*